TO

THE DONORS OF THE

MATTATUCK FOUNDATION

Preface

THE contents of the following pages rest upon certain fundamental assumptions; that the meaning of life is of vital interest to us all; that poets are our most beloved and persuasive teachers of what makes life significant; that the poets who are truly great are those who have presented the largest area of human experience most justly and powerfully; that they have become immortal because their ideas and ideals run accordantly with the deepest currents of our belief in the realities of life; that they teach by what they say, but more by the characters they create, the principles they take for granted, the moods they communicate.

The poets considered in this book belong to the ages and have contributed most to the mind and soul of Occidental civilization.

To *Advance* I wish to express gratitude for permission to use 'My Personal Experience,' originally appearing in that paper under the title 'Guidance through the Poets.' I am indebted to The Macmillan Company for allowing me to quote from John Masefield's 'Essay on Poetry;' also the quotations from Alfred Austin, W. G. de Burgh, A. C. Bradley, A. E. Housman, and the translations of Lang,

Preface

Leaf, and Myers are inserted with the consent of the same publishers. In the study of Homer I have used for the most part Bryant's metrical translation, supplemented by the prose translations of Lang, Leaf, and Myers. I have followed Blackie's rendition of Aeschylus in Everyman's Library. Lucretius is presented through the prose of Munro and the verse of Mallock; Virgil through the metrical translation of Theodore Williams (permission by the Harvard University Press and Houghton Mifflin Company). Dante's thought I find to be most clearly presented in Norton's prose.

I feel under especial obligations to Miss Henrietta C. Bartlett for reading in manuscript the chapter on Shakespeare, and to Doctor Richard H. Clapp for reading practically the whole of the manuscript. Their suggestions were most wise and valuable.

CHARLES ALLEN DINSMORE

NEW HAVEN, CONN.
January 18, 1937

Contents

ix

Contents

THE GREAT POETS
AND
THE MEANING OF LIFE

Introductory

THIS volume, to which I invite the reader's interested attention, has grown out of a series of lectures on the *Spiritual Content of Literature*, which I have been giving for the last sixteen years in the Divinity School of Yale University. In the lectures Dante, as the supreme poet of Christianity, occupied the greater portion of the time; the other poets were mountains on the horizon. Here I bring them into the line of the Great Succession. It has been a most enviable fortune to be able daily to enter the company of the Immortals and hold high converse with them.

Decline of Cultural Studies

To all lovers of literature the crowding out of cultural studies in our institutions of learning in order to center the attention upon so-called practical and vocational subjects is a matter of real regret. The ease and suddenness with which it has been done is an indication of the fever and impatient haste of these days. Certainly 'the world is too much with us'; we are dull to the wonder and glory which beset us on every side, and fail of those

I

glimpses which give to life its richest meaning. We are so obsessed by the concerns of the immediate present and future that the past is too often forgotten and the treasure-houses in which its dearly bought wisdom is stored are neglected. The deeps of human nature change not at all, nor the essential forces working in all problems, and the lamp of experience is still the best light safely to guide our feet.

Mankind has been on this planet for a long time and has learned many lessons. To this bewildered day of ours, so engrossed in quick expedients and unpremeditated experimentation, these books bring the gold refined in ancient struggles. These poets, from Homer to Shakespeare, are exponents of the wisdom of the major civilizations of the world. They interpret to us, in terms of life, what men have most valued. We speak of illustrious poets as seers; often they claim the title, but what they really do to us is to make selected experiences so vivid that we see their inner meaning and their relationship to the harmony of the whole. The poets are not the bringers of new tidings, but are the revealers of the significance of things and of deeds; they bring the obscure to light and say the commonplace with radiant energy. Their glorious platitudes are what men need if they would keep in the paths of true progress.

The Great Books

It is reported that Daniel Webster in his closing years, appraising his contemporaries, remarked, 'I cannot think of Henry Clay sitting down of an evening to read the great books.' Henry Clay was one of the ablest and best beloved of the political leaders of our country, yet it is a severe indictment to declare that one does not readily associate him with the chief fountains of intellectual light and power. For great books are something more than Milton's famous description would indicate — 'the precious life-blood of a master-spirit embalmed and treasured up on purpose to a life beyond life.' The covers may suggest the embalming process, but not the pages. A good book is a master-spirit speaking to us, uttering what is deepest in his own nature, voicing the soul of the epoch to which he belongs. As we read the veil of the intervening centuries grows thin, and we commune with an Immortal face to face; his glory and strength come into us, we see the world through his eyes and add to our consciousness new areas of experience.

Thus the enduring books offer a sure way of escape from the tyranny of the present. Often on opening the morning paper we are reminded of the first assault on Dante's senses as he entered the Inferno; the air was filled with 'strange tongues, horrible utterance, words of woe, accents of anger, voices high and faint, sounds of clapping hands, making a tumult which whirls away in that air which is forever dark.' The more we are devoted to the service of our generation, the more we need occasionally to flee to the high mountains of past achievement for peace and invigoration. Ancient sorrows comfort us, and battles long ago induce serenity. Even the *Inferno*, looked at through six hundred intervening years, seems quite comfortable and reminds us of many acquaintances. Contemplating Clytemnestra and Iago through the enchantments of art, our minds are purged and elevated by the strong emotions of tragedy. An ancient Hebrew poet, writing about the influence of the men who tower above their fellows, declared, 'The mountains shall bring peace to the people.'

The poets included in this volume have proved, through many centuries and civilizations, their ability to gird the mind with strength. In the literature of power they stand pre-eminent. Their heroes and heroines are of the old, heroic breed, they criticize life by displaying its possibilities of valor and virtue; their passions are elemental and universal, their speech is that of the gods in stateliness and music. Reading them we receive the inflowing energy which comes from intellectual and moral exaltation.

These poets bring us close to the Everlasting; to that Ultimate Reality which acts upon us as truth and beauty and goodness. They have been so fortunate in their hour, so delicate and comprehensive in their genius, that through them the eternal truth and beauty break in splendid utterance. Something greater than themselves is communicated. A word which pays no homage to the sun has made itself heard in the courses of history. Men have always needed, and they need today, wisdom, power, inspiration, the permanent. Where shall we find the heights of detachment, the fountains of strength, the voices of approved authority, except in the books which stand unimpaired by the sure test of the centuries? Where is the changeless in a changing world, if not in the verses of our supreme poets, who are abiding because they are identified with the Everlasting and flash forth some aspect of his glory?

A Personal Experience

When Dante would make his perilous journey through Hell and Purgatory he chose for his guide, not Aristotle, a philosopher, nor Aquinas, a theologian; but Virgil, a poet. In Purgatory, when uncertain of the way, they were directed by two other poets — Sordello and Statius. It has been suggested that by these selections Dante intimates that poets are the most inspiring and universally effective helpers in the way of life. To test this theory by my own experience I opened the book of my memory and found this written:

It was in a village school and through its reading book that I first felt the power and joy of poetry. The hours in the schoolhouse were very long, the studies dry and resented, the benches hard, and the only interesting thing in sight which it was entirely safe to lay hold of was a soiled reading book. What a treasure it was, though I little suspected it then! The best that man had thought or said lying within easy reach, offering the only escape from arithmetic and boredom, and having the attractiveness of forbidden fruit. I thought I was evading study, and lo! I was unsuspectingly absorbing the essence of many studies. Into my unguarded mind slipped images of beauty and ancient truth; dormant senses were quickened by the bright ring of words, aspirations toward the heroic were enkindled. The lines of 'Horatius at the Bridge,'

'Marmion,' 'Barbara Frietchie' had the sound of trumpets in them; they quickened the imagination and called to valor with infinitely more power than a lecture on ethics. A few years later, when the long, long thoughts of youth began to ferment within me, I found in the old veneered secretary in the living-room at home a little blue and gold copy of *Longfellow's Poems*. Longfellow may not have been as eminent a poet as our fathers thought, but he certainly gave memorable expression to our common longings and finer sentiments. He sang into my mind the conviction that life is not an empty dream, that the mills of God grind slowly, that Excelsior is the motto for ambitious youth, and that cares have a way of folding their tents like the Arabs. This was more effective than many sermons.

About this time there came to our school a young man, fresh from Dartmouth, whose own mind had only just been opened to the glories of literature. Glowing with enthusiasm for the strong gods of English speech, he taught an elementary course in English literature. For him the golden haze was over the whole landscape, and he made us see what he saw, and feel what he felt, as he led us into a land entirely new and full of wonder. My untutored soul stood erect when John Milton's mighty organ note of song went crashing through the chambers of my imagery. Vividly I beheld Satan striding over the burning marl of Hell. As though present, I listened to the arguments and felt the passions of the magnificent debate of the devils in Pandemonium. Milton may have put no facts into my mind, but he smote it with magic power. Through his harmonies I felt the beating of an heroic spirit, and there came a sense of something great and noble which gave life meaning, color, and glory. Oh, the wonder and the dream of those days! Poor in pocket, I was traveling in the realms of gold, and it was great education; a sure defense against the dark and savage wood, the leopard, the lion, and the wolf.

The method by which this eager teacher inspired me with a love of literature is not without suggestiveness. As the course was a brief one he could give no more than one or two lessons on Milton, but instead of assigning to the class long sections to read, and then quizzing us about the classical allusions and the meaning of words, thus turning a thing of inspiration into a source of information, he told us the story, read with infinite zest the significant portions, and made us keen to know more of this fascinating author. Consequently, *Paradise Lost* was not a task, a thing to evade; it was something magnificent to appreciate. I did not study it; I enjoyed it, I declaimed it, I felt it, and then I bought it! How crammed with educational material was the hour given to rhetoricals! Our imaginations took to themselves wings and flew from the little Vermont village to the Roman forum, and the chills ran down our spinal columns as we saw Virginius hold his dripping whittle in the face of Appius Claudius. We were in Scotland with Montrose, and saw the white plume of Navarre wave over the field of Ivry. We absorbed literature and history in those resonant hours, and felt 'culture hum.' Ambition was stirred, and we dreamed dreams of greatness.

The Great Poets and the Meaning of Life

In school and college I learned just enough of Homer, Virgil, Aeschylus to dimly apprehend that those obscure sentences which I was trying to translate and construe concealed fire; but as my attention was fixed on the grammatical constructions, little of the splendor shone through. To use one of Dante's similes, it was like fire moving beneath alabaster, and the alabaster seemed very thick. Not until many years later, when I could, with good conscience, read the classics in translations — read them as poems and not as ponies — did I catch their vision and feel their passion, though of course I lost much of their peculiar beauty.

Both in school and college Shakespeare had a not unimportant place, but in my school days he did not stir me as Milton did. I suppose that to a boy's immature mind sonorous rhetoric is more appealing than lines of subtle meaning and beauty. In college I was most fortunate in having an excellent teacher in elocution, and through him I felt the spell of our greatest poet. Poetry, to be appreciated, must be brooded over, that one may catch its spirit, and spoken, that one may note its melody. To bind a poem on a dissecting table in the interests of philology and grammar is profitable for exactness in scholarship, but it is not the best method of cultivating esthetic appreciation. In my elocution class I doubtless tore the dramatist's passions to tatters and split the ears of the groundlings, yet I learned by heart his finest passages; I caught their music; I had glimpses into subtleties of character, the terrors of conscience, the tragic forces of life, the radiance which shines from lofty virtue. I felt and dimly perceived a greatness which transcended my understanding.

Up to this period the poets had been to me men who unveiled the significance and beauty of a world not seen with the eyes; they had been trumpeters summoning to high endeavor. Now they became guides in a time of bewilderment, for I was entering that chill land of religious doubt when one casts off his childish notions of the faith and meets the challenge of maturer knowledge. It was a time of groping and of real intellectual distress. Tennyson performed for me and for my generation a priestly service by showing how to keep one's hold on the supreme affirmations of religion while still retaining one's intellectual integrity. More than any other he made me realize that there is more faith in an honest doubt than in half the creeds, that our little systems have their day, and that the wages of virtue are not dust. Whittier also cleared away many difficulties by revealing the great distinction between the inner spirit of religion and its creedal and ecclesiastical shell. While these poets told me no new thing, they clarified truth and made it effectual: they kept me close to the elemental and the everlasting.

Then for many years poets and poetry occupied a very small portion of a life absorbed in other interests. But 'the feet of the gods are shod with wool,' and they have a habit of stealing into the inner chamber of one's life, unexpected and unobserved. Thus casually and permanently did Dante enter into my life. One summer day, during vacation, when I was past the middle milestone on life's way, I took from a friend's library a copy of Longfellow's translation of the *Divine Comedy*. I had no knowledge of Dante and I disliked long poems, but the day was hot, the *Inferno* seemed an appropriate title, and this was the only book which was the least intriguing. Finding a shady spot in the woods, I opened the volume most indifferently. But indifference soon changed to absorbed attention; I felt the spell of an imperial mind cast over me. Like Pascal, instead of a book I had found a man. What the greatest of the Christian poets has done for me in the years since then it would be impossible to tell, but he revealed to me the spiritual secret of the Middle Ages, and thus enlarged the boundaries of my sensibilities; he cut a new gate into the spiritual world and showed me life *sub specie aeternitatis*: he visualized truth and related it in a vast system; he quickened my mind and heart by the intensity of his imagination, glowing in sentences of radiant energy; he gave me a standard of literary judgment which has proved helpful in these times of the Great Confusion.

I have not mentioned the English Bible because the magic of its diction did not burst upon me suddenly as did the genius of Milton and Dante. Brought up in a religious home, familiar with the Scriptures from childhood I paid as little attention to their peculiar beauties as I did to the beauty of the sunlight. Yet even in boyhood certain passages in the book of Revelation gave me a strange thrill. In the primary school of our village the daily session was opened by a chapter in the New Testament, each pupil in turn reading a verse. Consequently, each of us had a Testament, with print so fine that only young eyes could attempt it. In the weariness of the long hours I occasionally turned its pages, because there was nothing else to do. I distinctly remember how for several days the vivid pictures of the apocalypse fascinated my imagination — the stately tragedy, the tremendous judgments, the blazing, Oriental glories of heaven, the sonorous music of the sentences were wonderfully impressive. Years later, when I was a lad of sixteen and had united with the Church, I felt, as a matter of duty, that I should become acquainted with my Bible. I looked upon it as a guidebook written to give explicit directions concerning this perilous way of life in which my feet were planted. But one Sunday afternoon, as I was reading the first chapter of Genesis, I felt strangely stirred by the sublime simplicity of the thought, and the majestic music of the lines. It was great poetry — truth shaped and colored by the imagination. Certainly it was not a scientific account of creation. Closing the book, I went out for a walk. I seemed to be exalted above myself, and the world was beautiful.

Only in mature life did the divine, serene beauty of the sayings of Jesus disclose themselves to me. Probably I was too familiar with them, but gradually I have seen that Jesus is as truly the fulfillment of the Hebrew poetic genius as he is the fulfillment of its aspirations after righteousness. He thought intuitively, as a poet thinks. The grace of his sentences is as divine as their truth. As we read them in our authorized version they have the balance and the cadence of poetry. They state the truth with wondrous lucidity, and yet with a rhythm that conveys the emotion which belongs to the truth.

Quite apart from their religious consolations and enlightenment, the Scriptures have taught me the value of simplicity in thought and speech; they have taught me that the heart apprehends Reality as well as the brain, and that moral truth comes to its full power in the rhythm of its utterance. It is truth plus beauty which make words immortal. The more intimately I know the English Bible, the more I am amazed at the sublimity of the Hebrew poetic genius, and the peculiar ability of our English tongue to convey its thoughts and passions in undiminished grandeur.

This is my tribute to the poets with whom my spirit has held high adventure; they awakened and have nourished in me the most precious, the most terrible gift I possess, the Imagination — the source of all rapture and trembling; they have made me vividly aware of a glory that is in the world and a significance that is in common things; they have discovered to me shining ideals and disclosed a world of realities which are abiding and beautiful amid all the fluctuations of fortune; they have widened my sympathies and enriched my feelings, lifting me into the High Mood; they have put a philosophy in a sentence, or an unforgettable picture, and made duty seem a privilege; they have opened wide gateways into a realm of peace.

The Poets Selected

The civilization in which we live draws from two main cultural sources — Greece and Palestine. From one comes strong inspiration in art, science, philosophy, letters; from the other the main ideas and motives of our faith. In the centuries which record our history, three poets of superlative power and excellence have interpreted the essential spirit of the ancient, the medieval, and the modern worlds — Homer, Dante, and Shakespeare. They are the sovereign and permanent monuments of these epochs. Philosophies, histories, treaties are forgotten, modified, or rewritten, but the poets abide. They present fundamental and universal emotion truly, and their beauty of form is an antiseptic against which time cannot prevail. The three poets mentioned are supreme; they are the authoritative voices of great epochs and reveal the inner spirit of the times. A great book is more than the 'life blood of a master spirit embalmed and treasured against the life beyond life'; it is more than a great man speaking. In an immortal book we hear the sound of a vast multitude, the voice of many waters. It is an epoch disclosing its secrets and its faiths. Therefore these three must be included in any attempt to apprehend life more comprehensively through the poets.

Aeschylus finds a place because his was the first and most powerful voice in Greece to affirm the moral structure of life when that marvelous people awoke to full self-consciousness. Sophocles was the more complete artist, Euripides is more appealing to our modern feeling, but to me Aeschylus is a mightier oracle.

After considering life from the Greek point of view, we shall pass to the next dominant civilization, that of Rome. Rome was not rich in poets of spiritual insight, but Lucretius was a seeker after ultimate truths, and presents a view of the cosmos which gave him peace and ecstasy. *De Rerum Natura* is the most monumental poem skepticism has produced, and certainly has a place in a discussion of the meaning of life as interpreted by the poets. Virgil does not rank with the supreme Three, yet he was a very great poet and has expressed the noblest ideals with which imperial Rome rationalized her conquests. The medieval world is represented by Dante, 'The voice of ten silent centuries.' The multiplicities and complexities of the modern world are mirrored in Shakespeare.

The reader will doubtless be surprised to find the Bible included in a study of the world's greatest poems, but I hope to show that it is a world epic in a sense which can be applied to no other book.

Use of Translations

It is appropriate to say a word regarding the use of translations. In the good old days, which we are accustomed to think of as abounding in leisure, the study of Greek and Latin occupied the central place in the curricula of our colleges, and Hebrew was diligently taught in theological seminaries. As a result, the number of those who could read the classics in the original tongues was considerable. Today the ancient languages occupy a very subordinate place in our schools. If the treasures of the ancient world are to have any influence, they must be conveyed through translations or not at all.

In this there is, of course, a real loss. The peculiar melodies of verse and felicities of phrase cannot be perfectly reproduced. But I believe this loss may be exaggerated. The greatest poems deal with what is universal in experience and in passion, and every developed language is fitted to reproduce these ideas and emotions with fidelity. Our English Bible is a translation. Its thoughts do not sound to our ears as they did to the ancient Hebrew, but all that is important and eternal is expressed according to the genius of our language. Neither thought nor emotion suffers in its full utterance through an alien tongue, but not an alien heart. The loving toil of generations of scholars has perfected the medium through which thoughts and emotions of other days are domesticated in our minds — emotions and thoughts which are common to us all. Goethe did not state the case too strongly when he said: 'I honor both rhythm and rhyme, by which poetry first became poetry, but what is genuinely and deeply effective, what forms and advances us, is that which remains of a poet when he has been translated into prose.'

Emerson's testimony is even more familiar. In his Essay on Books he writes:

> I do not hesitate to read all the books I have named, and all good books in translations. What is really best in any books is translatable; any real insight or broad human sentiment.... I rarely read any Greek, Latin, German, Italian — sometimes not a French book — in the original which I can procure in a good version. I like to be beholden to the great metropolitan English speech, the sea which receives tributaries from every region under heaven. I should as soon think of swimming across Charles River when I wish to go to Boston, as of reading all my books in originals, when I have them rendered for me in my mother tongue.

A similar confession we have from Mr. Justice Holmes, the solidity of whose scholarship none will call in question. His biographer tells us that he was fond of uttering a dissent when reminded that he had the reputation of reading the classics in the original. With a 'pony,' he vowed, it was not so difficult. 'But,' he once added solemnly, 'I always qualify that against the Day of Judgment; for I read in the original only the purple patches. Suppose on the Judgment Day *le bon Dieu* were to call me up and say, "Now tell us, Holmes, very briefly, what you got out of Socrates in the original that you would not have got out of a translation." And then I should have to say: "But, Milord ——"'

These masterpieces of world poetry will be studied as documents of the spirit, not as works of art. The purpose is to learn what they have added permanently to the world's intellectual and spiritual treasure; what they communicate to us of truth and power. We shall search for the real beliefs of these authors, not in the nature of the gods they worshiped, in the popular faith of their times, or even in their own professions. What they believed without question is what they assumed and made structural in their dramas and epics. There we shall find what they thought of the quality of life, the nature of its powers and its legitimate ideals.

Poets as Interpreters

MANY are the men who assert their claims to lead humanity through the wilderness to safety and fullness of joy —
scientists, sages, economists, theologians, philosophers —
but the poets differ from all other leaders in very decided
ways. The scientists are expert teachers in physical things,
and we follow them obediently to the very limits of their
domain, but they deal with facts and forces, not with
spiritual values. The sages are wise men whose feet are
guided by the lamp of experience, therefore they look
toward the past and condense the wisdom of many into
an arresting sentence. The economists help us in our
fortunes, but not in our prayers. The theologians rear
monumental systems confidently and with infinite care,
yet these highly articulated structures we use, not as
pillars of fire and cloud, but as milestones, marking
humanity's progress. The philosophers make the strongest
claim to fullness of wisdom. Plato, Aristotle, Kant, Hegel,
what leaders in the realm of the spirit have names more
authoritative than these? Yet their insights have proved
more valuable than their logic. Plato is sovereign of them
all because of the range and profundity of his poetic

17

imagination. Science, proverbial wisdom, systems of thought belong to the realm of knowledge, and knowledge passes away; poetry belongs to the realm of values and is less affected by the flight of time.

When Job was in trouble three philosophers came to him with their little systems of thought. Poor comforters, indeed, they proved to be. The philosophy of the friends having failed, the poet assumed his priestly office. No more than the philosophers could he understand the mysterious ways of the Eternal, but he felt vividly the majesty of the power and the minuteness of the wisdom of the Creator. Of these he sang, and with the vision of the greatness of his God came the peace of reconciliation.

In What Manner do the Poets Help Us?

Of course we must distinguish between the greater and the lesser poets; the poets of mood and the poets of vision. Some are but idle singers of an empty day, troubadours who shorten the way of our pilgrimage by their songs. We read them for pleasure, or to feel more intimately some phase of experience. It is the immortals who

> ... get at the strength of things,
> And fearlessly make strong songs of it,

of whom I write.

The greatest poets without exception have been great men. A mighty torrent does not rush from a six-inch pipe; neither has the Creator yet sent a stupendous truth into the world through a trivial mind. A plain man, but never

18

a plain mind, may utter momentous things. Aeschylus, Dante, Shakespeare, Milton, Goethe were comprehensive, balanced men; a civilization or an epoch could speak through them. Consider for a moment the mental endowment which a laureate of England declares is required to treat worthily a great theme:

> Lofty imagination, a full and flexible style, a copious and ready vocabulary, an ear for verbal melody and all its cadences, profound knowledge of men, women and things in general, a congenital and cultivated sense of form — the foundation of beauty and majesty alike, in all art; an experience of all the compassions, yet the attainment of a certain majestic freedom from servitude to these; abundance and variety of illustration; a strong apprehension and grasp of the Real, with the impulse and power to transfigure it into the Ideal, so that the ideal shall seem to the reader to be the Real.[1]

Coleridge states the same thought more simply: 'No man was ever yet a great poet who was not at the same time a great philosopher, for poetry is the blossom and fragrancy of all human knowledge, human thoughts, human passions, emotions, language.' Lamb in his essay on 'The Sanity of True Genius' says:

> So far from the position holding true that great wit has a necessary alliance with insanity, the greatest wits, on the contrary, will be found to be the sanest writers.... From beyond the scope of Nature if he summon possible existences, he subjects them to the law of consistency. He is beautifully loyal to that sovereign directress even when he appears most to betray and desert her.

[1] Austin, Alfred, *The Bridling of Pegasus*, p. 23.

Again, the great poets are keenly sensitive men, reacting powerfully to influences which would be unnoticed by coarser natures. 'Our difference in wit,' declares Emerson, 'appears to be only a difference in impressionability, or power to appreciate faint, fainter, or infinitely faintest voices and visions.' It is this delicacy of the mental antennae, quivering to many and far vibrations, which gives the poet his insight and power. Poets reveal to us something we should otherwise miss; they uncover a real world of beauty and significance; they apprehend qualities in objects and situations which are veiled to ordinary mortals; 'they lift the veil from the hidden beauty of the world and make familiar objects be as if they were not familiar,' to use the fine words of Shelley. This delicate sensitivity causes them to feel keenly, to react powerfully, and the strength of their emotions quickens all their intellectual processes. They seem to be lifted above themselves, and thought and emotion become inspiration, art, poetry.

The poets help us because they are mightily concerned with life. Poetry is a revelation or an interpretation of life in some of its aspects. Great poetry interprets life greatly: it reveals experience in amplest range, comprehensively and profoundly. The most gifted and permanent leaders of the world have all had the minds and usually the methods of poets.

The philosophers talk about life, the poets represent it; they reveal it in its extreme moments, its raptures, its tragedies, its victories.

The poetic material is not only life, it is life as it is

known to the emotions. The treasures of the mind are constantly changing, the emotions are universal and enduring. Knowledge passes away, but

> Love is Love, though Latin swords be rust,
> . . . .
> And Care is still but Care,
> Though Homer and his seven towns be dust.

It is because the poet feels more intensely than other men that he is capable of great and authoritative expression. Meeting us through the emotions, he imparts to us the 'feel' of life: he makes us realize its quality; he holds the cup to our lips and lets us taste its bitterness and its joy, its worth, and its vanity.

We have been saying that the supreme poets have been balanced and full-orbed men, uncommonly impressionable, and therefore vivid, emotional, and communicative of emotions, so that we feel what they feel. Moreover, we have stated that their material is life in its many aspects and in its intensest moments.

We wish now to call attention to the fact that the poets use superior methods to communicate their facts and truths. They put thought in its most persuasive form, for we not only understand the idea, we see it. They think in pictures and speak in metaphors. They make truth visible through action, story, symbols, and all concrete forms. They give us not only the idea but the quality and values of truth. They make it musical in the cadence of the lines. Schopenhauer may give us the ideas and moods of pessimism, but how easily Shakespeare brings the same

cold mist of depression over the mind in that sad funeral
march beginning

> Tomorrow, and tomorrow, and tomorrow,
> Creeps in this petty pace from day to day
> To the last syllable of recorded time,
> And all our yesterdays have lighted fools
> The way to dusty death. Out, out, brief candle!

The abstractions of the philosopher cannot so readily
give the 'feel' of an idea, and even the novelist cannot put
so much in so little space with such enchantment of
language. There is a natural magic in true poetry which
opens the mind and heart that thought may enter with
least opposition. The watchers at the gate are charmed
and the messenger easily enters the throne room to plead
his case. Said an eminent scientist after reading an equally
eminent poet, 'He told me what to do in a way that persuaded me to do it.'

The moralist may expound the moral law, but the
dramatist seizes the precise moment when sin and its
consequences come together — the tragic moment when
sin is revealed in its results. Thus the moral order becomes
visible in its most impressive character. We see it living
in men and women: we feel its inviolability in the calami-
tous event.

The historian may bring out the central truths of a great
epoch, but he deals with many facts and forces; the central
issues are often obscure; many years, perhaps centuries,
intervene between the original cause and its tragic results.
But a drama has an organic unity which is impossible to
history; it presents more directly than history can possibly

do the fundamental issues, unencumbered by the incidental and irrelevant. Thus its truth comes with greater clarity and power. The epic poet shows us life as lived by heroes, life magnified by perilous adventure; the lyric poet sings the truth, passionately and musically. Remember 'there is often more truth in a legend than in a document.'

We have shown, have we not? that the greater poets are qualified to be helpers of all pilgrims on this strange journey of life because their ideas are directly related to life and its experiences, they present their thought in concrete words and vivid imagery, they appeal to the emotions and the imagination as well as to the understanding, they bring vast areas of experience and passion to an instant focus, they use language, in their best moments, in its most perfect form, making true Arnold's bold assertion that 'poetry is the most perfect speech of man.' They lift us into the High Mood, they give us power and the vision splendid.

Before proceeding further it may be well to say a few words about a blighting and contagious heresy which has done much to devitalize modern poetry. The heresy is this, that poetry has nothing to do with morals; teaching is not its office. This would have astonished the Greeks, who used Homer as an effective teacher of the heroic qualities. The Athenian State made the tragic poets a chief means of inculcating reverence and virtue. The Romans placed the study of poetry central in their educational system, and Virgil's dominant purpose in his epic was to make the Romans fit for the vast responsibilities of empire. Dante made himself lean for many years that he might make manifest the way of life. Unless six hundred years of celestial blessedness have greatly tempered his fierce indignation, he must have said, when he heard it whispered in heavenly circles that Italian critics are now saying that the poetry of the Divine Comedy is confined to its lyrics, 'Such sentiments should be answered, not with words, but with daggers!' Shakespeare did not aim at moral instruction, but he criticized life by showing the radiancy of Virtue and the ugliness of vice. Professor Garrod, in his recent lectures at Harvard University, claimed that this divorce of poetry from the chief concern of life goes no further back than the French decadents. The poets have always believed that their office was to make men better. The highest human interests are Virtue and Truth. 'When we wish to communicate with one another we do not keep our best speech for second-hand interests.' The poet teaches truth and virtue better than any others. Poetry disconnected from moral ideas dies from being uninteresting. There is a deal of truth in Matthew Arnold's familiar statement, 'The noble and profound application of ideas to life is the most essential part of poetic greatness.' And Emerson testifies that 'the high poetry of the world from the beginning has been ethical.'

Let us remind ourselves of John Morley's comprehensive definition of literature: 'Literature consists of all the books — and they are not so many — where moral truth and human passion are touched with a certain largeness, sanity, and attraction of form.'

They Claim Superior Illumination

It is interesting to note that the poets have usually asserted an illumination superior to that of other men. 'Poetry is ever thought,' says Bacon, 'to have some participation in divineness.' The Hebrew prophets were convinced that Jehovah was making revelations of his mind through them. The Greek poets felt the presence of Apollo, and their habit of invoking the Muses was more than a convention. They were mastered men, and their enthusiasm was the energizing of the god within them.

Modern poets are not less confident. Wordsworth, when wrapped in the 'serene and blessed mood,' affirmed that he saw into the life of things. Tennyson says of the poet:

> He saw through life and death, through good and ill,
> He saw through his own soul,
> The marvel of the everlasting will
> An open scroll
>
> Before him lay;...

Browning gives this witness: 'For I know I myself have been aware of the communication of something more subtle than the ratiocination process when the inspirations of genius have filled my soul to the depths.' Masefield, in his stimulating lecture on poetry, strains language to emphasize this element of vision. 'I believe,' he says, 'that the best poetry has always been a radiant perception of the Life of the Universe, of its Persons, its Powers, and its Laws, as they exist eternally, and that the mood of poetry in which these are perceived is an undying mood, existing eternally, as the Heart of Life, and that true poetry, which is living that mood, and setting down of its truth, is essentially eternal, too.'[1] He affirms that to the high poets, great men living in a great time, poetry is an illumination, but to lesser poets, in shallower times, poetry seems to issue only from talent directed by good taste and care. To A. E. Housman poetry is a much simpler thing. In his lecture on 'The Name and Nature of Poetry,' delivered soon after Masefield's noble pronouncement, he declares, 'Poetry is not the thing said, but the way of saying it.' The poet has no higher task than to 'transfuse emotions.' Mr. Santayana, poet and philosopher, bridges the chasm between the two; 'Poetry as form expresses thought which is sensuous and ideal; inwardly it is a Light, a Fire, a glimpse of the divine, a momentary harmony.'

This much I think we must grant, that the poetic mind is delicately sensitive to the finer influences, is intuitive in its workings, and is strongly imaginative. Such a mind, brooding and reasoning, will be rewarded by a flash of insight, 'a steady contemplation of all things in their order and worth.' As a matter of fact the spiritual leaders of the world have been men of precisely this type. This faculty of imaginative insight poets share with the leading philosophers and scientists. They may penetrate no more deeply into Reality than other men of sovereign endowment, but they behold more radiantly, feel more intensely, and communicate more powerfully. Also they are more companionable.

[1] *Poetry*, by John Masefield, p. 6.   A most suggestive treatment.

Poets as Interpreters

Our more thorough knowledge of the workings of the mind explains to a degree the astonishing certainty with which the poet-prophet speaks. In men of genius the connection between the conscious and the subconscious mind is very close. A thought dropped into the 'Deep Well' seems to be taken up subconsciously, analysed, arranged, clothed, and then projected, vivid and complete, into consciousness. The thinker is unaware of any volition on his part. The vision, the word, has come without his seeking. Nietzsche, whose mind was assuredly impressionable, intuitive, and imaginative, thus describes the actions of the mind at this moment of vision:

> If one had the smallest vestige of superstition left in one, it would hardly be possible completely to set aside the idea that one is the mere incarnation, mouthpiece, or medium of an almighty power. The idea of revelation in the sense that something which profoundly convulses and upsets one becomes suddenly visible and audible with indescrible certainty and accuracy describes the simple fact. One hears — one does not seek; one takes — one does not ask who gives; a thought suddenly flashes up like lightning, it comes with necessity without faltering. I have never had any choice in the matter.

The experience of every poet and prophet in the Great Mood has been like this. The daemon, the god, the Eternal is revealing his truth through him. Therefore poets and prophets speak as oracles, with authority and not as the reasoners.

The Authority of Great Poetry

Upon the following consideration I wish to lay especial emphasis. The authority with which the true poet and seer speaks does not rest solely upon the definiteness and keenness of his mental impressions: it reposes on a basis as infallible as our mortality can find, namely, the age-long experience of the race. When a thought sinks into the deeps of the mind it awakens primitive instincts, associates with itself habits old as humanity; the essence of long tradition, ideas, images, words, symbols, inherited from an immemorial past, these swept together by the transforming imagination come rushing upon the poet's vision. The authority of great poetry is that it is the utterance of primal instincts and the treasured experiences of the race. This is why the poets are safe leaders; they walk in the old paths, they sing the results of

> ... old, unhappy, far-off things,
> And battles long ago.

Their wisdom is not the outcome of their individual reasoning, it is the distillation of racial memories. The reader of the pages which follow will find these world poets expressing the common faith of their day; they deal in platitudes familiar to the wayfaring man. Because they are so elemental they have universal appeal; they sing of passion, its ecstasies and its terrors; they sing of sin and inevitable retribution; they sing the everlasting distinction between good and evil; they sing the glory of love and man's 'unconquerable will.'

28

Poets as Interpreters

It is instructive to note that a poet in his ordinary moods, when he speaks according to his reason and his prejudices, may be a most unwise counselor. He is no nearer truth than others in his conversation and his letters, but when he puts on his singing robes, when the divine madness possesses him, he utters *himself*, and therefore something universal. The fountains he draws from are not those of his individual idiosyncrasies; he draws from old experience, the instincts and traditions of the race, the universal and tested. Newman and Whittier are far apart in their creeds, but in their poetry they come near together. Poets agree in everything except their theories. Fundamentally they are alike; from their many torches comes one light and heat. Better than other men they separate the essentials from the non-essentials. It was the poet-prophets of Israel, not the priests, who disentangled the simple way of religion from elaborate rituals, and first announced the unity of history and the redemptive energies latent in suffering love. Poets unveil the hidden beauties of the world, the glory of the ideal, and the meaning of disaster. They have been the chief inspirers of the generations calling them to virtue, heroism, and love. Apollo, god of light, god of music, has made them oracles of the law of harmony which creates the beauty and rhythm of the world, which gives art its proportion and conduct its moderation.

The great poets interpret the innermost spirit of their country and civilization to the world. Through them the ages understand each other and bring the race of men to sympathy and unity.

The Great Poets and the Meaning of Life

Every nation gives peculiar honor, a rare homage, to its poets. They are the glory of a people, the exponents and measure of a civilization. In their magic words the thoughts of many hearts are revealed. They unveil the wonder of the world, give enchantment to the common place and significance to the trivial. They sense the eternal rhythm that runs through all things. In briefest manner and in clearest light they reveal life in its extreme moments and make visible realities not seen with the eyes.

The great poets stand on our horizons like mountain ranges, sublime witnesses to the fiery convulsions of other days, now calm ministers of peace.

HOMER: *What He Believed and What He Valued*

THE influence of the *Iliad* and the *Odyssey* upon the Greeks was profound. For some ten centuries these minstrel songs were more to the Greek-speaking people than was the Bible to the Christians from the fifth to the fifteenth centuries. And even during the last four hundred years, since the Old and New Testaments were translated into the vernacular, the Scriptures have not enjoyed the monopoly of attention which the Greeks accorded to Homer. In those early days 'poetry was power.' It sang the glory and the tragedy of life into the hearts of the people. Through the wisdom and valor of glittering and very human heroes, children received the ideals which were to govern them. Yet we must remember that their ideas of the nature of religion were far different from ours. The good to them was not love of one's enemies, purity, and humility, but hospitality, valor, and the thrill of joyous living.

To the immense vogue of Homer recent excavations in Egypt bear remarkable testimony. Here Homeric papyri are so plentiful as to become a nuisance. 'The great popularity of the bard is indeed one of the chief trials of the excavator's patience. He sees an extra large literary fragment emerging from the soil, and wonders for a brief moment what new treasure he has found, but ten to one it is only old Homer again.' When the future excavator digs into the refuse piles of our buried cities will he be troubled by the abundance of Bibles, or copies of Shakespeare? More likely he would turn up a mass of comic supplements, had not a wise Providence taken thought that the paper be fragile. To call Homer's epics the Greek Bible is not incorrect, for here a great people beheld eminent virtues personified and the issues of life interpreted. To these writings they appealed to settle controversies, and from them their civilization took its tone.

Who Was Homer?

To us these epics mark the beginning of the literature of the western world. They are the rosy-fingered dawn of our modern day. But sunrise to us means sunset to others. The extraordinary perfection of the diction and meter of these poems shows them to be the ripe fruit of a matured civilization, the noble spirit of a vanished epoch. Like the *Divine Comedy*, they mark the end of one world of thought and the beginning of another. The question inevitably arises, Who was Homer? The answer is most unsatisfactory. He may have been an individual, or a syndicate: a person or a personification of a group of singers. In Greek tradition he was a blind poet of extraordinary endowments, who sang his lays of the Trojan war to court and banquet hall:

> Seven cities claimed Homer dead,
> Where Homer living begged his bread.

This tradition, floating down through many centuries, is unsubstantiated by a single historical fact.

The old belief that the *Iliad* and *Odyssey* were the creation of one supereminent genius, named Homer, met with a rude shock in 1795 when Friedrich August Wolf revived the startling theory that the epics were not the work of one author, but of many rhapsodists. He not only relegated the poet Homer to the realm of myth, he even denied that Troy had existed. In his opinion Pisistratus, tyrant of Athens, in the sixth century B.C., caused the primitive lays of a legendary war to be arranged and unified into a standard text.

Some thirty years after the publication of these iconoclastic views, a boy, Heinrich Schliemann, was born in Germany. As a lad his youthful imagination was kindled by the hero-tales of Homer. Teaching himself Greek, he worked diligently in trade that he might obtain money to find Troy, and prove the veracity of the *Iliad*. Having accumulated large wealth, he spent from 1870 to 1882 in finding the city, which he identified at the modern town of Hissarlik, a hundred miles northwest of Smyrna and three and three quarters miles back from the Hellespont. Digging down through a series of cities, he found what he believed to be the ruins of ancient Troy, but Dörpfeld has since established one higher up in the same tell as the capital of Priam. This has a wall twenty feet high and sixteen feet thick, yet not so extended as Homer would have us think. In one passage he indicates that fifty thousand troops were sheltered within Ilium, but the exhumed city could not have held more than three thousand. Numerical accuracy is not the habit of poets.

Having recovered the site of Troy, and the richly treasured tombs of the Mycenean kings, we are still debating the wonderful epics, how they came to be, and who wrote them.

Gilbert Murray in his *Rise of the Greek Epic* propounds a theory in line with the position taken by Wolf. According to Professor Murray, both the *Iliad* and the *Odyssey* are traditional poems — poems written, not by a single author, but by many generations and many authors. He holds that the Trojan War marked the end of the Heroic Age, and subsequent bards, steeped in its traditions, sang its deeds. Such was their racial genius that they created an epic style, an epic meter, almost an epic language. In the sixth century B.C., Pisistratus inaugurated the Panathenean festival. During this great festival, which occurred every four years, he commanded the *Iliad* and *Odyssey* to be recited. As there were many and varying songs, and differing accounts of the same event, he caused the poems to be put in order and a standard text to be made. Mr. Murray goes so far as to suggest that the task was performed by Kynaithos and his school of rhapsodists. These took the dispersed, varying, and divided parts and wove them into a unity, connecting, altering, adding as suited their necessity. The text, however, remained fluid, additions and subtractions being made as late as the third century B.C. According to this theory Homer is a mythical ancestor of poets, their genius personified.

But the weight of authority inclines to a more conservative position. There is a general agreement that the tradition of a Trojan war rests upon an historical foundation. The siege is supposed to have occurred about the year 1200 B.C. It may have been caused by a chivalrous purpose to avenge a breach in the code of honor, but it is more probable that this is another case of a struggle for a commanding commercial position and the markets of the world. It hardly could have lasted ten years, for it would have been impossible to hold the army together for so long a time. (A non-Homeric account of the war by one Diktys, A.D. 300, of Crete, preserved in a Latin translation of a Greek original, states that the war lasted through two winters and the siege through only one).

As by the eighth century B.C. the epics had become famous, the poet who conceived and most nobly sang this story of the war must have lived in the ninth century. His *Iliad* in its main substance and arrangement became a living thing. Later rhapsodists expanded and modified these poems into the epic we now have. 'That the *Iliad* as a whole,' writes Andrew Lang, 'existed long centuries before Pisistratus is the hypothesis least fertile in difficulties.'

The *Odyssey* from its mellower tone, its maturer thought, its more artistic construction was once thought to be the work of Homer's old age. Recent scholarship is inclined to date the *Odyssey* one or two hundred years later than the *Iliad.* But many protest. To them the difference in matter, style, and tone is no more pronounced than the difference between *Paradise Lost* and *Paradise Regained.*

Whether an individual or a school, it is permissible to speak of the creative mind out of which the poems came as Homer, and we shall so use the name. My conviction is that although groups of poets may possess common characteristics of thought and expression and establish a tradition, yet the unity of these epics, their sustained grandeur of style, the remarkable nobility and genius of the informing spirit, attest the action of a supreme mind. Important movements in economic and political matters may originate with the crowd, but when we come upon lofty achievements of the mind it is well to search for the solitary thinker.

This general consensus of conservative opinion that the poet Homer lived not later than the ninth century B.C. suggests a very interesting comparison between the *Iliad* and the earliest portions of the Old Testament in point of style and outlook on the world. It is a prevalent opinion among Hebrew scholars that in the latter part of the ninth century, about 825 B.C., a first-class story-teller in Judah arranged the traditions and documents of his people into a continuous narrative — the first attempt at history, as far as we know, ever made. This author, called 'J' by the scholars, was probably very nearly contemporaneous with Homer, and his style in simplicity, directness, rapidity of movement is strikingly similar to that of the poet. His God, too, is intensely individual, and walks and talks with men. A conspicuous difference is that Homer is beautifully rich in descriptive adjectives and epithets, while 'J' omits them almost entirely. His lines have not the glamour of Homer's, but as a story-teller he is not inferior.

There is also an interesting parallelism between the events they record. Herodotus places the Trojan War about 1250 B.C.; Professor Murray fixes the date about 1200 B.C.; later writers incline to 1192 as marking the outbreak of the war. While exact knowledge is lacking, it is quite probable that when Agamemnon was having his troubles with Achilles, Moses was having his difficulties with Aaron and the golden calf. These conjectures may not be important, but they are not without value to those who study the contrasted genius of nations.

The Art of Homer

The spell which the poet has cast over his readers can be analyzed but imperfectly. Keats, when he first opened Chapman's translation, sat up all night reading, and in the morning struck off an immortal sonnet to express his wonder — a new planet had swum into his ken, an ocean of feelings, sublime and sparkling, was disclosed to his astonished eyes. Even the dullest reader of Homer must discern how fittingly 'wide expanse' and 'pure serene' describe the horizon and the atmosphere of the *Iliad*. A true instinct made Keats compare the epic to a star and an ocean, for the spirit of the open air is here, and a brave new world, with the dews of morning upon it, and radiant goddesses with lucent eyes talk with men. The characters are of heroic proportions, the emotions displayed are common in all ages, and the language is natural, flowing, direct, and simple. The poem has the qualities so well summarized by Matthew Arnold — rapidity of movement, plainness of thought, simplicity of expression, and the grand manner. By the grand manner he is supposed to mean that the poet in describing common things does not become commonplace, and that in depicting heroic deeds and emotions the language rises adequate to the theme. Everywhere a kingly mind shines through the words, sustaining and irradiating the sentences. Energy and poetic fire keep the story alive and splendid.

From these general characteristics, if we pass to detail, we are impressed by the exceeding vividness of the poet's imagination, his lucidity of mind. Here is no vague impressionism; every scene is clearly conceived, and the characters are so real that they are accepted as historical persons. When a warrior falls we see precisely where the blow struck, we hear the crash of the bronze armor. Sometimes it is almost too vivid for our modern stomachs. When we actually see Patroclus dragging Thestor by his jaw over the rim of his chariot, as a fisherman pulls a sacred fish from the sea, leaving him as he fell, our qualms compel us to ask ourselves whether we are more civilized, or simply more effeminate, than the men of old. The poet makes a scene real by making the details clear. Would he make us see the Greek army, he does not give us a general description, but takes us with Agamemnon as he goes through the host and talks with the different chieftains. Would he make us feel the shining glory of Achilles on the field of battle, he lets us see the glittering armor as the hero puts it on piece by piece.

He reinforces the reader's imagination by the naturalness, abundance, and appropriateness of his similes; they rest the mind in scenes of strenuous action, they furnish a background to make us realize the situation more keenly.

Homer fills his pages with a bewildering variety of men and women, yet he conceives each so clearly as an individual that with an adjective or phrase he makes them live. An epithet flashes a picture — bright-eyed, 'well-greaved,' 'far-shadowing'; or a single sentence reveals a character — 'A man who lived by the side of the road and gave hospitality to all'; 'One omen alone is best, to fight for native land'; 'She laughed with her lips, but there was no joy in her face.' These lift the veil and we see deep and far. He lived in an age less sophisticated than ours, and looked at the world with young eyes, with a childlike as well as a lucid mind. Like the Old Testament narrators, he takes us to a scene and leaves us. He trusts the reader to see and to feel, and does not, like the writer of today, dim the picture with his private fancies, or linger on its emotional implications.

His skill as an artist, as well as his magnanimity as a man, are revealed in his treatment of Helen. How shall he picture to his reader the most beautiful woman in the world? He is too wise to attempt to describe the

> ... face that launched a thousand ships,
> And burnt the topless towers of Ilium,

therefore he tells of the effect her glorious beauty has upon others. To the old men of Troy, her natural enemies, she seemed as an immortal goddess, and they ceased to wonder, after they had seen her, that the young men should for her sake suffer hardship.

Neither did he condemn her, for she was but the instrument of Fate. Her lament over the fallen Hector is one of the finest passages in the *Iliad*, and goes far to rehabilitate her character in the reader's estimation.

It is a mark of genius that out of meager experience it can open up great spaces of thought and emotion. From a little it gets much. The period covered by the *Iliad* is very short — about fifty days; the subject is extremely limited — the prowess of warriors, funeral games, friendship and feasting, the wrath of a man and the beauty of a woman. But with this trivial material the poet portrays most powerfully those emotions which are common to people of all epochs and countries. They are of the stuff of which all timeless literature is made — love and loyalty, courage and fear, gladness in simple things, the tragedy of death. Homer knows the stern joy which warriors feel, but with greater sympathy and with equal power he discloses life's pathos. The parting of Hector and Andromache, and Priam pleading for the body of his son from the bloody-handed Achilles, are high points in literature.

Civilizations change, centuries hurry by, but man's elemental emotions change as little as the sunshine or the sea. Homer has seized the passions of a border warfare between semi-barbarians and has portrayed them so powerfully and in verses so nobly beautiful that they remain an enduring revelation of man and a supreme monument to poetic genius.

The Permanent Spiritual Values of THE ILIAD

In searching for the enduring spiritual verities which Homer apprehended and enforced, we must constantly bear in mind that moral instruction was far from his purpose. These lays were sung at banquets and festivals to give pleasure to the hearers and renown to the minstrel. Their aim was delight, not instruction. Occasionally the poet may utter some favorite conviction, either by way of comment or through the mouth of one of his characters, but primarily he is reciting a story, old in the tradition of his people, and to this he must be true.

This absence of didactic purpose is most fortunate for us, because what one really believes is not what he consciously teaches, but what he assumes as self-evident. We are surer of our assumptions than of our arguments. We proclaim and defend our opinions; we act upon what we really lay to heart. The foundations show what one solidly trusts; the superstructure reveals the quality of one's imagination and understanding. Not only does the lack of a didactic intention disclose the poet's deep convictions, it also brings us near to the confident beliefs of his hearers. He is reciting to please his audience and his tale must conform to their presuppositions. He must do no violence to their instinctive beliefs, if he is to be popular. Therefore in an accepted epic courses the spiritual life blood of a race. In the presuppositions of the *Iliad* we have more than the convictions of Homer; we have the ideals and principles of many generations of the most gifted people of antiquity.

The plot of the *Iliad* is so familiar that we give only a meager outline to refresh the reader's memory.

According to the ancient legend, Paris, son of Priam, had violated the laws of hospitality and the home by carrying to Troy Helen, the wife of his host Menelaus, King of Argos. Eager for vengeance, the Grecian chiefs, under the command of Agamemnon launched a thousand ships, and when the story opens, the Greeks have been beleaguering Ilium for some nine years, with varying fortunes. Homer chooses for the theme of his song the fateful quarrel between Agamemnon and Achilles, which took place the last year of the siege.

The daughter of Chryses, priest of Apollo, has been made captive and is held by Agamemnon as a prize of war. The priest offers a ransom which the warrior gruffly refuses. In revenge for the insult to his priest, Apollo for nine days sends his pestilence-bearing arrows upon the Greeks. The seer Calchas declares that the god will not be appeased until the King restores to the aged priest his daughter. At this announcement

> Wide ruling Agamemnon greatly chafed.
> His gloomy heart was full of wrath, his eyes
> Sparkled like fire.

To save his people he gives back the 'fair-cheeked maid,' Chryseis, and for recompense takes Achilles' prize, Briseis, whom that impetuous warrior dearly loves. In sullen anger Achilles retires to his tent and refuses to have further part in the war. From that hour the siege goes against the Greeks and they are driven to their ships. The misfortunes of battle exhaust Agamemnon's anger, and so clear his vision that he perceives his folly in alienating Achilles. In a council of war the King acknowledges his fault and offers to make restitution to the offended chief:

> With gifts of priceless worth. Before you all
> I number them — seven tripods which the fire
> Hath never touched, six talents of pure gold,
> And twenty shining caldrons, and twelve studs
> Of hardy frame, victorious in the race.
> .   .   .   .
> Seven faultless women skilled in household arts,
> Damsels in beauty who excel their sex.
> These I bestow and with them I will send
> Her whom I took away — Briseis, pure.

Moreover he grants Achilles the first chance in the division of the spoils of Troy; he may choose twice ten young Trojan women, beautiful beyond their sex, save Helen; he may become Agamemnon's son-in-law, having the choice of the King's three daughters, and as dowry, Agamemnon will give seven cities with thronged streets.

Three of Achilles' dearest friends bear to him this offer of reconciliation, but the sullen warrior refuses to be appeased:

> I leave him to himself
> To perish. All-providing Jupiter
> Hath made him mad. I hate his gifts; I hold
> In utter scorn the giver.

The battle is renewed, and the Greeks are driven to their ships by the Trojans, who attempt to set fire to the fleet. Patroclus, Achilles' most cherished friend, can endure inactivity no longer, and tearfully asks leave to don Achilles' armor and lead his myrmidons to the relief of his comrades. Permission being given, he performs prodigies of valor, carrying the battle to the very walls of Ilium, where he is slain.

Achilles is inconsolable at this loss. Love clears his eyes to the evil consequences of his conduct. He will re-enter the conflict and avenge his friend:

> Along the beach the great Achilles went,
> Calling with mighty shouts the Grecian chiefs.

They assemble in council, and Achilles renounces his enmity. When Agamemnon presses the offer of gifts upon him, he treats it as a matter of small importance, but this the judgment of the King will not allow. The maid Briseis is restored, and with her are given the presents Agamemnon had promised. Putting on his glorious armor, Achilles leads the attack, defeats Hector, and drags the body at his chariot wheels. With the pathetic picture of the aged Priam begging the corpse of his son and bearing it away by night from the tent of the victor, the poem ends.

The theme of the story seems to be lust and war; nevertheless it plunges immediately into a consideration and solution of one of the world's profoundest spiritual problems. If Homer correctly reveals the principles and dispositions which bring Agamemnon and Achilles together, he throws light on the most insistent spiritual

44

question which has engaged the attention of the Church —
the question of the forgiveness of sins. How can there
be reconciliation after wrong has been done? The organic
idea running through the *Iliad* is a deed of sin, its fright-
ful consequences, and the way of reconciliation. Sin,
Retribution, Reconciliation, are the theme of the *Iliad*;
they are the theme of our greatest literature; they are the
heart of the message of religion. Homer answered the
question of reconciliation between two strong and in-
temperate men by telling a simple story and by following
his own deep instinct. Theologians have formulated the
identical principles in terms of philosophic dogma. The
moods and the actions which will heal the breach of sin
between two persons anywhere will be identical everywhere. No preacher has treated more vividly than Homer
the source and nature of evil, the sure retributions which
follow wrongdoing, and the constant elements which enter
into forgiveness and reconciliation. His theme is Achilles'
wrath, to Greece the direful spring of woes unnumbered,
which sent to Hades many a valiant soul. The consequences of the wrath were that Achilles sulked, Patroclus
was slain, mighty chiefs were untimely killed, and the
Greek cause came to the verge of disaster. Reconciliation
comes when atonement has been made, the past forgotten,
and the two commanders are again allies in the same cause.

Homer assuredly does not think of sin in terms congenial to a modern theologian. Sin, as we meet it in the
first instance, is a violation of sacred taboo. Agamemnon
has injured the priest of Apollo, and as penalty the god
sends his arrows of plague on the army. In the light of his

punishment the King sees his folly, repents of it, confesses
it, and makes restitution. Then spontaneously the Greeks
do two other things which are suggestive: they clean their
camp of all pollutions, and they sing a hymn in honor of
the offended god. Thus in the very first pages of this most
ancient literature, we have a witness to the instinctive
feeling that sin is polluting and its stains must be washed
away, for the high gods are pleased with cleanliness.
Therefore the baptisms and lustrations in all faiths. Then
immediately after they have done all they can by way of
restitution, the Greeks sing a hymn to Apollo. When we
remember how the Church in all her various formulations
of the doctrine of forgiveness has ever taken pains to
make clear that God in being merciful has also been just,
and that in pardoning he has in no way diminished the
sanctity of his righteous law, this instinctive act of
homage becomes significant.

It is to be observed that the evil thing here is not the
inhumanity of Agamemnon in holding Chryseis, the
priest's daughter, in foul bondage, but his contempt of
the priest. Having made restitution and performed the
purifying rites, the King has cleared himself as regards
the sun-god. His relations with Achilles are not so easily
restored. The methods the poet used to bring about complete reconciliation throw a flood of light on the principles
which enter into all atonement, whether human or divine.

The word the Greeks used to express wrongdoing of
every kind was 'ἄτη with its verb. The root meaning is
'befooling.' Sin is blindness; folly, delusion. And so
clearly is punishment bound up with folly that the Greeks

included both under the one conception personified as
Ate. They were also very human in laying the blame for
their folly on the gods, and yet they had a real feeling of
human responsibility. When Agamemnon woke to his
blindness in alienating Achilles he exclaimed:

> But it is not I who am the cause, but Zeus and Destiny
> and Erinys that walketh in darkness who put into my soul
> fierce madness on the day when in the assembly I, even I,
> bereft Achilles of his meed. What could I do? It is God who
> accomplisheth all. Eldest daughter of Zeus is Ate who
> blindeth all, a power of bane: delicate are her feet, for not on
> earth she goeth, but walketh over the heads of men, making
> men to fall; and entangleth this one or that.

In another mood he freely takes the blame upon himself.
In the first pages of the *Odyssey*, Zeus tells how the gods
feel about it:

> How strange it is that mortals blame the gods
> And say that we inflict the ills they bear,
> When they, by their own folly and against
> The will of fate, bring sorrow on themselves.

Automedon, the son of Diores, very forcibly gives the
answer of all practical men to this question of fate and
free will: 'Yet verily these issues lie in the lap of the gods;
I too will cast my spear and the rest shall Zeus decide.'

If Homer as well as the moderns is confused about the
original source of evil, he is perfectly clear in stating what
it is that brings a man back to sanity. In the disasters
which befell his army, Agamemnon realized the true
nature of his folly. Always, both in literature and experience, it is a vivid knowledge of the consequences

which brings a man to himself. It is 'the woes unnumbered,' falling thick upon one's self, which opens eyes blinded by passion. To win back the allegiance of Achilles, Agamemnon acknowledges his fault, sends three friends to offer reconciliation, and promises to restore Briseis pure, and present other gifts in munificent abundance. He not only repents of the wrong; he confesses it. He does more; he renders every satisfaction in his power to atone for his offense. Obstinate pride keeps Achilles stubborn. But the death of Patroclus, his dearest friend, reveals to him his great folly. Renouncing his enmity, he joins the battle and brings victory to the Greeks. He has taken the three steps essential to all complete reconciliation — repentance, confession, fruits meet for repentance or expiation (*confessio, contritio, satisfactio*).

Now let us consider some further assumptions which the great poet makes. Our modern historians lay heavy emphasis on geographical and climatic conditions as affecting the course of history, but in both the Scriptures and in the *Iliad* the great man is always the hinge upon which events turn. The Bible interprets history in the light of the character and deeds of significant men. In Homer the fate of nations hangs on the temper of one man. Achilles sulks and the battle goes against the Greeks, the hero takes his proper place, and the cause prospers. The power of the individual looms large in the ancient books.

Because so great a weight of responsibility hangs upon the hero, he must not, like Agamemnon, act peevishly, putting his selfish desires above the interests of the cause, or, like Achilles, nurse his private grievance to the detriment of his comrades. Unity through self-subordination is one of the chief lessons of the *Iliad*.

To what extent Homer accepted the shining gods of Olympus can never be known. Their names and stories were a common tradition of his times, and he used their dramatic possibilities to the full. But he places them in too many ridiculous positions to have held them in genuine reverence. He could not very well escape being a polytheist. As he looked out over his world, he saw the beautiful and the ugly, the forces which hurt, the forces which help; he saw evidences of freedom and evidences of irresistible fate, of order and caprice. Many wills seemed to be working on human destiny. To personify these forces, the gods and goddesses would be as congenial to his mind as to that of his race. Yet, amid the infinite variety, superior minds discerned a unity, or semblance of order. Zeus, the highest One, prevailed in the councils of the gods. From his rod there was no appeal, and the weight of his government was ultimately for righteousness. He was not indifferent to the deserts of men. He approved of Hector because he was the only man in Troy who never was scornful of Helen; though believing she should be given back to the Greeks, he fought because honor compelled him. Even in those early times, a noble and pondering mind never wholly interpreted the world scheme by what his eyes saw. He instinctively directed the light of his own nature upon what he experienced, and therefore he had faith that valor, justice, and mercy were dear to heaven.

Just here we come to a very significant fact. Although the Greeks, like all primitive peoples, deified the forces of nature, their deities did not take the form of somber monstrosities like the gods of many nations, but were radiant ones, dwelling in ethereal light, graceful, amenable, capable of unquenchable laughter. Thus they shine in Homer, giving to his pages a charm which could not come from Egypt or Assyria. What Homer did believe very sincerely, and assumed as the controlling principle of his epic, was a truth which later emerged as the master conviction of the Greek civilization, a conviction which gave form and glory to Greek art, set the standard of its oratory, gave strength and beauty to its literature, and would have saved the people from the errors which destroyed them, if they had possessed sufficient self-control to put it into practice. The motto, 'Nothing too much,' comes as near the secret of the glory that was Greece as can any single statement. This sense of proportion gave to their art its severe and graceful beauty, and to their literature its classic restraint. The Greeks had their shrines and rituals for the gods of high Olympus, but their sovereign creed was balance, proportion, the supremacy of reason. This structural faith of the men of the higher consciousness in Greece will later find clear expression in their dramatists. It is interesting to observe that Homer assumes this principle as a matter of course; it moulds the whole fabric of his song, and tempers the glowing energy even of his words.

Achilles might well be angry at the indignity heaped upon him, but his wrath was excessive, and this excess was the source of all the woe which followed. Patroclus would have lived had he obeyed the injunctions of Achilles, but his impetuous valor carried him beyond bounds. Achilles acts as a hero when he avenges his friend, but when in his uncontrolled fury he drags Hector in the dust, he brings reprobation on himself. The cause of every woe from the sin of Paris to the fall of Troy was excess of passion. The poet nowhere explicitly utters this truth, but he assumed it, and it is the organic philosophy of his epic.

A most powerful factor of any drama or epic is the background against which the action is set. This determines the final impression of the whole. In the *Iliad* the immediate scene is radiant with the glitter of the ocean, the glory of heroes, the beauty of women, the splendor of gods and goddesses; but the background is Fate, and because Fate dooms most men to sorrow, and all men to death and to the weakness and shadows of the underworld, therefore life is sad and human glory is futile and tragic. Zeus may be the father of the gods and the king of men, but even he is subject to the superior authority of Fate. The most memorable expression of this subordination is found in the issue of the rivalry between Hector and Achilles. Zeus was favorable to the Trojan, but Fate decreed otherwise. The two warriors are confronting each other for the final combat:

> Then the Father hung his golden balances, and set therein two lots of dreary death, one of Achilles, one of the horse-taming Hector, and then held them by the metal and poised. Then Hector's fated day sank down, and fell to the house of Hades, and Phoebus Apollo left him.

In the very years when Homer was painting his brilliant picture of heroic adventure shadowed by impending doom, over in Palestine were men of a loftier spiritual consciousness who saw life against a background that was at once righteous and compassionate. And because their God was good and supreme life had meaning and the future held a great hope.

To Homer life had no ultimate meaning. Man might have a moment of joy, but in the end his soul went to the house of Hades, wailing its doom — Hades, the land of wraiths and weak shadows, of which Achilles said he would rather be a plow boy on earth than rule over the realms of the dead.

The note of hopeless sadness is constantly uttered throughout the *Iliad*. Finely has Glaucus expressed this mood: 'As is the race of leaves, so is the generation of men, the wind casts some leaves to the ground, others the flourishing forest brings forth when spring has come, so is the generation of men, one is born and another passes away.' 'There is nothing,' declares Zeus, 'more wretched than men. Nothing of all things that breathe and move on the face of the earth.' Achilles is evidently of the same opinion, for he asserts, 'The gods have decreed that wretched mortals should live in sorrow, while they themselves are free from care'; and again: '*Two* urns stand upon the floor of Zeus filled with his evil gifts, and *one* with blessings.' How keenly Homer felt the pain and the pathos of existence is revealed in the touching scene between Hector and Andromache. Here he faces life's most perplexing problems — the suffering of the innocent for the guilty, needless sorrow, death to no purpose, the destruction of home and country — and the poet can offer to the weeping wife no consolation save that of duty bravely done. One must carry on. Fortunate is the man, if with inevitable evil he gets some good in life.

Although life is full of sorrow and death certain, Homer does not give himself over to pessimism. He does not wail or whine. Everywhere he strikes the heroic note. Because life is short, live nobly!

> O friends, be men, so act that none may feel
> Ashamed to meet the eyes of other men.

Nowhere is this heroic mood more finely expressed than in these words of Sarpedon: 'For assuredly ten thousand fates of death do every way beset us, and these no mortal man may escape or avoid. Let us now go forward, whether we shall give glory to other men or they to us.'

The remarkable feature of the *Iliad* is that against this dark background of death and futility the poet communicates a zest for life. Generous hospitality, kindness to strangers, heroic valor, are so touched by imagination as to be glorious. This goodness of life is not directly expressed in words but is communicated through the radiancy of the characters. Achilles may be impetuous, but he is magnificent in energy, a god in action, sublime in generosity. The very fact that he chooses to go into the battle for the sake of honor, even though he knows that by so doing he will go early to the eternal shades, makes him appear all the more heroic. The *Iliad* leaves the reader not in a mood of pessimism, but with a stouter and more generous heart, inclined to respond to Hector's cry, 'Play the man, my friends, and be mindful of impetuous valor.' Life is short, death is certain, Hades a land of gloom, yet carry on with high courage.

The poet felt deeply the pathos of life, its brevity, its pain and frustration: he also felt the glory of wisdom and the heroic deed. Homer took a noble view of life because of the essential nobility of his own mind. It is his glory, both as a poet and as a man, that, dealing with a sordid story of lust, bad temper, and savage butchery, he nowhere makes vice attractive, but brings the reader into sympathy with beauty, fortitude, and magnanimity.

Besides the heroic mood there is a virtue which is not explicitly taught but is a spirit of life in the poem itself. This virtue is the inestimable one of sympathetic understanding. Homer was a Greek, singing to a Grecian audience the exploits of their national heroes, yet he so tells his story that his hearers understand and sympathize with Hector; they feel the sorrows of Andromache; they take the part of Priam, pleading for the body of his dead son, as against Achilles. This ability to see events through the eyes of one's enemies is quite characteristic of the Greek genius. We find it in her historians, her dramatists, and her poets. It is significantly absent from early Hebrew literature. The books of Ruth and Jonah stand in lonely isolation in the Old Testament. The first record of sympathetic imagination in the stream of literature which forms our culture appears in Homer, and his subtle and indirect persuasions to toleration form one of the noblest spiritual values of the *Iliad*.

In this epic we have no lofty insights into the ultimate meaning of things, but we do have our attention focused powerfully on certain virtues of enduring worth, courage, magnanimity, fortitude, moderation, tolerance. Above all we feel the radiant energy of a strong and noble mind unveiling to us unfamiliar beauty, and inspiring our hearts to valor. But of high religion as the modern mind conceives it — communion with the eternal spirit, humility, the spiritual worth of personality, unselfish service in the interests of a high ideal, and a pure heart — of these there is no hint. The good life here is not love of one's enemies, purity, and humility, but beauty, courage, and the thrill of joyous living.

THE ODYSSEY

I find my biography in every fable I read.
EMERSON

Doubtless many minstrels in many songs celebrated the return of the various Greek chieftains from the Trojan War. Only one account survives in completeness, the tale of the wanderings of Odysseus, called by us the *Odyssey*. The *Iliad* is a collection of the legends of war; the *Odyssey* is an artistic fashioning of the legends of the sea. It employs that ever-interesting theme, the man who came back when all supposed him dead. 'The *Odyssey*,' says Mr. T. E. Shaw in his recent translation, 'is by its ease and interest the oldest book worth reading for its story, and the first novel of Europe.'

55

The authorship is much in dispute. Some wise men still hold the traditional view that it is the work of Homer in his old age, for the tempo of the poem is slower than that of the *Iliad*, the tone mellower, the artistry more delicate. Others, because of its more varied and harmonious language, its maturer thought, claim that this epic is later than the *Iliad* by several generations. The question, though interesting, does not concern our present purpose. The unity of its authorship and the genius of a single creative mind are very evident. This poet we call Homer. Doubtless he used earlier legends, moulding and adding to them, and the date assignable to the construction of the poem as a whole cannot be later than the year 750 B.C.

This date catches our attention, and recalls our analogy between Homer's epics and the earliest continuous narrative of the Old Testament. We have noted how nearly contemporary was the Trojan War with the Exodus (the thirteenth century B.C.), and the author of the 'J' manuscript with the great poet of the *Iliad*, both living in the ninth century B.C. About a hundred years after 'J,' a writer in northern Israel composed a similar chronicle from the standpoint of his time and people. He is known to scholars as 'E,' and his period as about 750 B.C. Like the difference between 'J' and 'E' is the difference between the *Iliad* and the *Odyssey*. In the latter works, the conceptions of Deity are less anthropomorphic, and creative energy has checked its fires and developed its art.

The Hebrew writers were as good at story-telling as their Greek contemporaries; indeed, they excelled in intensity and restraint of imagination. They also had a greater respect for their material, incorporating it in its original form, instead of shaping it in their own moulds of thought. Consequently they never attained the unity of style and the sustained diction of the Greeks. Their interests were different; the Hebrews were chiefly concerned with God and his character and will, the Greeks with man and his adventures. The heroes of the Pentateuch were Abraham and Jacob, obedient men; the favorites of Greek folklore were conquering men — Achilles, victorious in battle, and Odysseus, overcoming all obstacles by sagacity, patience, and fortitude. No more than the *Iliad* does the *Odyssey* have a loftier purpose than to tell a good story, but it is a good story according to the Greek idea, because its constructive thought is the triumph of the human mind over circumstances: Penelope keeping her integrity by patient endurance sustained by mother wit, and Odysseus actively confronting each danger.

The outlines of the tale are familiar. The Trojan War has lasted ten years. Now it is over, and Odysseus with twelve ships and some six hundred men launch their vessels for Ithaca. For three years the hero encounters incredible difficulties and suffers many things because of the wrath of Poseidon, whose son Polyphemus Odysseus had blinded. Then for seven more years he is held captive on an island by the enchantments of the nymph Calypso. The story begins with Athene calling the attention of Zeus to the injustice done Odysseus by his enforced bondage; Zeus sends Hermes to command Calypso to release her captive. She obeys and Odysseus continues his voyage upon a raft, which is soon wrecked in a storm, and he is thrown exhausted upon the shores of Phaeacia. In one of the most charming episodes of the poem, it is related how the maiden Nausicaa clothes him and leads him to the court of her father, the King. Before the court, Odysseus recites the story of his many experiences, and the King in his admiration gives him quick passage to his home in Ithaca.

But here, during the ten years of his absence, all has not been well. Believing him to be dead, many princes, attracted by the beauty, wealth, and power of Penelope, his wife, have come as suitors for her hand. Faithful to him and hopeful of his return, by shrewd devices she keeps from making a choice. Meanwhile the years drag on. Telemachus, Odysseus' son, now over twenty years of age, in despair at the wasteful orgies of the wooers, sails to seek of Nestor and Menelaus news of his father. After learning much of the closing days of the Trojan War and of the adventures of the Greeks, he returns home and meets his father, who in the disguise of a beggar is awaiting the opportunity to declare himself. The first twelve books tell the story of the experiences of Odysseus and Telemachus, the last twelve of the homecoming of the hero. They relate how at the palace only his faithful dog, whom he had left twenty years before, recognized him; how, being in the garb of a beggar, he was insulted by the suitors; how Penelope promised her hand to the one who could bend the bow and shoot the arrows of Odysseus; how the suitors failed, and then the hero bent the bow, shot an arrow through twelve rings set in a row, and in wrath turned the shafts upon the dastards until he had slain them all; how he was recognized by his wife, and established in his home and upon his throne. After toil and peril, rest and security have come at last.

The construction of the poem is admirable. Consummate skill is shown in weaving together the stories of the principal characters and in keeping the interest at a high pitch. But it is the meaning of the poem for human life which here concerns us.

A work of art is significant according to its meaning to the one giving it serious attention. Homer doubtless constructed the *Odyssey* to give pleasure to his hearers and to gratify his creative impulses. What further ideas were in the back of his mind, unperceived perhaps by himself, we do not know; but large numbers of competent readers have seen in his story a marvelously impressive allegory. As we meditate upon the legend, we seem to trace our own biography. Every life is like a voyage over a strange and bewildering sea. We are buffeted by storms, tempted by nymphs, and pursued by fearful monsters. Like Odysseus, we are beating our way over the deep in quest of security and peace, and like him we cannot in one decisive struggle win our victory and henceforth have rest. Life is a series of adventures, it is meeting each day the obstacles of the day. We live victoriously only by constant wisdom, courage, and patient endurance. And we can do this because there is something heroic in the human spirit.

The Great Poets and the Meaning of Life

An Allegory

Considered as an allegory, we classify it with the *Divine Comedy*, *Pilgrim's Progress*, *The Quest of the Grail*. But with this difference: These show the adventurous spirit moving out from home in search of a distant goal; the *Odyssey* is a story of a man from a far country who comes home.

How vividly and truly the main sources of danger are described! Who in youth has not been tempted to linger in delicious indolence with the Lotus-Eaters — 'men who make food of flowers'? The enchantress Circe has stations where she turns men into swine. The Sirens, too, lure voyagers to wreck by the magic of their songs. The safest way to escape is to stop the ears, or perhaps the strong cords of habit may hold one. Many and powerful ropes restrained Odysseus, but when Orpheus went that way he tuned his lyre, vanquishing the Sirens by a music sweeter than their own. Love of the highest is, after all, greater security than the restraints of habit.

Homer dares to give us the very song the creatures sang, and lo, it is the old song heard in Eden, and wherever men are tempted: 'Come hither and you will find both joy and knowledge.'

Baring-Gould tells us that the name 'Siren' means 'to whistle,' and infers that the wailing of the wind through the cordage, presaging shipwreck, gave rise to the legend.

The narrow and dangerous passage between Scylla and Charybdis has passed into a proverb, so typical is it of common experience.

Calypso represents in a somewhat different form the hindrances to progress on life's voyage. Her spell does not turn men into swine, or lure them by false promises of knowledge. She is a symbol of pleasure, offering immortal youth with all its satisfactions. But seven years of it leave Odysseus wretchedly bored and longing for home and peace.

One of the most powerful sections of the epic is the descent into Hades, in which we learn that the dead are without strength or intelligence unless they drink of the blood of sacrificial animals. So wraithlike and joyless are they that Achilles makes an exclamation which has become famous: 'Better be the hireling of a stranger, and serve a man of mean estate whose living is but small, than be the ruler over all these dead.' Two thousand years elapsed before Dante went into the eternal world. In the mean time Aristotle had lived and Jesus had taught the worth of the human spirit; therefore Dante found the distinctions between good and evil much more sharply drawn, and the souls of the redeemed, not gibbering ghosts, but pillars of fire, columns of splendor, too glorious for mortal eyes to discern their features. To Homer the laying off of the body had taken away the source of joy; to Dante the body was but a garment.

From this experience issues, quite incidentally, a principle which has loomed large in religious thinking. It comes in unobtrusively, but is a main part of the plot. According to the story, the misfortunes of Odysseus had been due largely to the wrath of Poseidon, who was pursuing him for the blinding of Polyphemus, Poseidon's son.

Tiresias, the prophet, gave him instruction in the method of propitiating the god. On his return home, Odysseus was to take a shapely oar and carry it until he reached a land whose men know not of the sea, nor had eaten food mixed with salt. This he would know when a traveler asked if the oar were a winnowing fan. Here he was to plant the oar, make fit sacrifices to Poseidon, and, returning home, offer hecatombs to the gods who held the open sky.

What instinctive belief lies under this strange commission? Planting the oar was not unlike Peary's action in planting the flag of his country at the North Pole. The explorer would do honor to his native land, extending its domain and power. So Odysseus lifted up the symbol of the sea in a country which knew it not, thus honoring Poseidon. This is a curious outcropping of the idea that has bulked so large in all doctrines of the Atonement, that forgiveness must be righteous, that in it there is an element of homage to a higher order. As in the *Iliad* the Greeks sang a song in honor of the offended Apollo, so here Poseidon outraged is propitiated by honoring his dominion. This instinct toward propitiation has a meaning which may not lightly be dismissed.

There are many poets — Goethe calls them 'the Lazaretto poets' — who are obsessed with a sense of man's failure. Homer was not one of these. Although he had a keen realization of the tragic aspects of life, he laid firm hold on something in the human spirit that overcomes the world. He believed in courage and makes us believe in it. He had confidence in human sagacity, and was assured that by wisdom and boldness man may sail victorious over life's stormy sea and find peace at last. The reader catches something of the indomitable spirit of Odysseus when he exclaims, 'Cheer up, brave heart, thou hast endured worse ills than these!'

And Penelope, she too conquers; not by bold decisive action, but by passive fortitude. Hers is the victory of those who by patience endure unto the end.

It is of more than passing interest to note that Homer, in accordance with both earlier and later tradition, placed the abode of the dead in the west. The Church has tried to reverse the symbol, and looks toward the east, finding in the rising sun the suggestion of immortal life. But in the World War the soldiers reverted to the instinctive habits of the race, and said of a departed comrade, 'He has gone west.' For thousands of generations, men have watched the sun go down in the splendors of the west and have had enkindled in them a sense of endless day, of a land which lies beyond the sunset and the baths of all the western stars. The Church may front the east to attest its faith in a future life, but the sunset has spoken its mystic language so long and powerfully that the primitive instinct prevails and men will continue to declare that the dead 'go west.'

AESCHYLUS: *His Genius and Spiritual Insights*

THE sixth century B.C. is one of the most important in the history of our race. In Asia it laid the foundations of great civilizations which have continued until this day. In that century Confucius was teaching in China, Gautama was stirring the soul of India, Zoroastrianism was experiencing a vigorous revival in Persia, and, according to the prevailing opinion of Old Testament scholars, the second Isaiah, the loftiest and most eloquent of all the prophets, was proclaiming his inspiring message in Babylon. In the latter part of the century Babylon fell, and with it the sovereignty of the Semites, and in Cyrus the Aryan stock attained a supremacy in world affairs which it has not yet yielded. Throughout Asia the sixth century marked the high tide of spiritual advance.

In Europe this strong pressure of the spirit took other forms. According to tradition it was in 510 B.C. that the Tarquins were banished from Rome and a republic, a form of government novel in those days, was established. In that same year in Athens the tyrants were overthrown and democracy was introduced into the courses of history.

It was in this century that Ionic culture spread in great waves to the mainland of Greece and stimulated the Greek mind to philosophy. In the succeeding centuries, the fifth and the fourth, Athens came to the fullness of her glory, but in the sixth century the intellectual awakening began, and in this century (525) Aeschylus was born. In that astonishing intellectual and spiritual quickening which appeared in Judah with the eighth-century prophets and spread during the sixth century through Asia and along the shores of the Mediterranean, a part of humanity threw off the primitive mind and took a long step toward maturity.

The Persian Wars

The immediate cause of this spiritual awakening in Athens was the Persian Wars. As the conquests of Assyria and Babylon awoke the prophets of Israel, as the defeat of the Spanish Armada aroused England to national greatness, so the terror of invasion and the joy of victory hastened the maturing of the Greek mind. At Marathon in 490 B.C. ten thousand Athenians, aided by one thousand of the soldiery of Plataea, defeated ten times their own number of Persians under Darius. This was no romantic foray like the siege of Troy; it was a desperate fight for existence. It seemed miraculous that a little city could withstand the most powerful dynasty of the world. Surely Zeus was mindful of the concerns of men; he was just and the defender of the weak. Ten years later, in 480 B.C., at Salamis the overwhelming might of Xerxes was broken by a little people apparently doomed. The spiritual ecstasy of this defeat of the supreme military force of the world marked a birthday in the mind of the Grecian people. They came to themselves. In art, in philosophy, in literature they threw off foreign influence. Thereafter they worked according to the dictates of their own genius. Seeing with their own eyes, they created enduring art and literature; thinking with free minds, they laid the foundations of science and adventured the quests and discoveries of philosophy.

Not the least remarkable was the emergence and sudden perfection of the drama. Four supreme masters of the dramatic art appeared in quick succession — Aeschylus, Sophocles, Euripides, and Aristophanes. The first three were unsurpassed as writers of tragedy, and the last was a master-writer of comedy. They found the mimic art a dithyrambic dance and chorus led by a single actor; they and their contemporary rivals touched this simple ceremonial with the magic of their genius, and it became immediately a thing of extraordinary power and beauty. Then the day of its splendor waned. Such dramatic genius did not appear again until Shakespeare came.

The first of this noble succession, and in many respects the greatest, was Aeschylus, a deep-souled, tempestuous man who went below the surface of life and grappled with humanity's profoundest problems. He was a man like Michael Angelo, a virile-minded Titan, yet extremely sensitive to the finer issues.

The Art of Aeschylus

Let us attend for a moment to what he did for the drama. Dionysus was the Greek god of wine and vegetation. In earlier times his worship was a revel accompanied by ecstatic song and dance, the leader telling the story of the God. As this story was both joyful and sad we have in the worship of Dionysus the germs of tragedy and comedy. It was all very simple, the revel of the country-folk in honor of the god who gave them wine and goodly fruits. But about 535 B.C., some ten years before Aeschylus was born, Pisistratus, tyrant of Athens, established the Panathenaic festival at which Homer's epics were recited, thus keeping alive the heroic tradition of the Greeks and furnishing fresh and familiar themes for the coming drama. He also built a theater south of the Acropolis, still standing in a modified form, erected an altar to Dionysus, brought his worship from the country to the city, and put it under the regulation of the State. This festival of the greater Dionysia was held in the spring, and its chief attraction was the contests of the poets for the tragic prize. The State selected the contestants, allowed each to put on four plays — three tragedies and a concluding satyr-play. The festival lasted three days and was considered an act of worship in honor of the god.

Aeschylus found a chorus of fifty, led by a single actor. The poet is credited with adding a second, thus increasing the possibilities of developed and dramatic action, and reducing the part of the chorus. When Sophocles added another actor, Aeschylus adopted the improvement. These players filled many rôles. Generally they spoke their lines, but sang the more lyrical parts as solos. Aeschylus replaced the old dancing meter by the stately iambic measure, and ennobled tragedy by his choice of heroic themes. 'He first,' says Aristophanes, 'built in strength the tragic phrase, and robed in stateliness what had been the tragic trumpery.' Because the characters represented were gods and heroes he is credited with introducing the mask and the thick-soled cothurnus to make the figures appear gigantic and awe-inspiring. Mr. Livingstone, in his most excellent volume, *The Pageant of Greece*, commenting on the long speeches which would be intolerably monotonous on the modern stage, where effects are produced by actions and gesture, affirms that the Greek actors perfected themselves in declamation, carrying the thought to the audience by exquisite articulation and cadence. The Greek drama is shorter than the English, and what it lacks in variety it makes up in greater intensity. The choral songs have different purposes. Sometimes they give the motive of the play, or create the atmosphere, or furnish contrast and relief.

In order to feel the full effect of the interpretation which is to follow, the reader should constantly bear in mind the great distinction between the ancient and the modern theater. In those early days the performances were solemn acts of religious worship. The altar of Dionysus was in the center of the dancing-place; his chief priest had the seat of honor. Like the passion plays at Oberammergau, the atmosphere was distinctly religious. The festivals were celebrated under the authority of the State to glorify the god and to educate the people. The most gifted poets offered their best work for popular approval, and a considerable number of citizens gave themselves to dramatic training that the plays might be brought out in a manner which would honor the god and be worthy of the State.

For one glorious period religion, education, and patriotism were harmoniously united in building up a unique institution. Since that day they have fallen apart. The drama is now a private enterprise; the controlling motive of the actors and producers is seldom the honor of God or the ethical education of the people, and the audience attends to be amused, not instructed. We have moved far from the day when one would think of affirming with Aristophanes that the vocation of the tragic poet is to preserve the State, and that it 'well profits the holy chorus to counsel and teach the city what is good.'

Judaism and Christianity are preaching religions. Prophet and preacher are the moral instructors of the people. In Greece the pulpit was the stage, and the chief ethical teachers were the dramatists. Our word 'pulpit' is from the Latin word *pulpitum*, which means the stage. When therefore a modern preacher stands in his pulpit to denounce the stage he is seething a kid in his mother's milk.

Lofty thought never had a nobler or more congenial opportunity to enter the public mind. Here from ten thousand to thirty thousand people are gathered under the blue sky in the presence of the shimmering sea and the majesty of the mountains, giving rapt attention as the most gifted poets the centuries have produced put in dramatic form the supreme crises of life, and the eternal principles which constrain conduct. Milton pays to the Athenian tragedians this tribute:

> What the lofty, grave tragedians taught
> In chorus and iambic, teachers best
> Of moral prudence, with delight received
> In high sententious maxims, while they treat
> Of fate and chance, and change in human life
> High action and high passions best describing.

Aeschylus was in no sense a cloistered poet. At thirty-five years of age he fought with conspicuous honor at Marathon and ten years later at Salamis. His genius evidently developed slowly, for he was forty-one before he gained the first prize in a dramatic contest, and he was sixty-seven when the *Oresteia*, his masterpiece, was produced. Two years later, in 456 B.C., he died.

As a poet he worked under the impelling inspiration of his genius rather than by artistic discipline. His rival Sophocles said of him, 'He did what he ought to do, but did it without knowing.' He draws his characters in large, strong outline; he creates an atmosphere which awes the mind with a sense of impending doom. He shows the terrors of conscience, not by tracing the stages of a deteriorating character, not by horrid dreams of blood upon the hands; he puts conscience on the stage as a brood of Furies. We do not infer retributive justice; we see it.

Aristophanes, in a description of a poetical duel between Aeschylus and Euripides, gives his impression of the former's style:

> What torrents of fiercely battling words shall we now have! They will shine like the glancing of helms in the

fight, waving with crested plumes on high! What high prancing charges of speech from the mighty master of mind! How he will shake his shaggy mane and bristle his bushy locks, knitting in wrath his terrible brows and roaring as a lion over his prey, hurling his huge jointed phrases about as if they were masses of timber from a ship's side, bound fast in bolts of iron: and then he will breath forth with a Titanic blast of his lungs.

And a modern writer, Frederick Harrison, declares: 'The *Oresteia* in mass, in intensity, in accumulated horror, in unity of idea and tone, and in statuesque sublimity of execution has never been equalled.' Swinburne goes even further in what seems extravagant praise when he says of the *Oresteia*, 'Probably on the whole the greatest spiritual work of man.' In the *Pageant of Greece* Mr. Livingstone writes, 'Nowhere else in literature is such audacious and colossal imagination, nowhere are we so constantly in the presence of the superhuman, nowhere is that superhuman so boldly and nakedly portrayed. Yet it comes without effort to Aeschylus; his unseen world must have been as real to him as the streets of Athens.'

The Spiritual Teachings of Aeschylus:
THE ORESTEIA

Of the seventy-eight plays written by the dramatist, whose titles have come down to us, only seven have been preserved. Of these *Agamemnon*, *Choephorae*, and the *Eumenides* are connected by a common theme. Produced two years before his death, they represent the dramatist's maturest thought. In this trilogy the tragic repercussions

of sin as it makes its fated way down through the generations, the inevitable clashing of right with right, the
exceeding folly of human pride, are set forth with a power
which thrills every reader who lends himself to its influence. The truths which the dramatist would enforce
he expresses partly through the direct affirmations of the
chorus, partly through the movement of the plot.

The form of the legend which Aeschylus used is as follows: Thyestes, son of Pelops, had wronged the wife of his
brother Atreus, who, pretending reconciliation, invited
the adulterer to a banquet at which he served the limbs
of Thyestes' own sons, 'a horrid stew.' The infuriated
father cursed Atreus and all his house. This terrible curse
hung as a doom over the family. One son of Thyestes,
Aegisthus, had escaped the fate of his brothers and was
received by Agamemnon, son of Atreus, who was apparently forgetful of the family feud, into the intimacy of
his own home. When the King sailed for Troy Aegisthus
avenged the slaughter of his brothers by living in adulter-
ous relations with Clytemnestra, the Queen. Agamemnon's
boastful pride had incurred the wrath of the gods, who
becalmed his fleet at Aulis. To atone for his sin Agamemnon had patriotically offered his daughter, Iphigenia, as
a sacrifice, and the fleet sailed. After ten years of siege
Troy was sacked and destroyed.

When the play opens Agamemnon is returning to his
home after his long absence, bringing with him Cassandra,
daughter of Priam, as his prisoner and mistress. Clytemnestra, burning with desire to avenge her daughter's death,
and angered by the presence of Cassandra, welcomes with

glittering hypocrisy the returning king and slays him immediately after he enters his house. Cassandra prophetically senses the 'horror and the snare of hell,' and approaches the palace with the prayer that her murderers may receive the judgment due their evil deeds. The scene closes with Clytemnestra in blood-stained robes boasting that full vengeance had been wrought for the victims of the past, and the chorus predicting that God would guide Orestes back to avenge his father's death.

The second part, *Choephorae*, opens with the return of the exiled Orestes, upon whom Apollo has laid the duty of avenging his father's blood. Clytemnestra, afflicted by hideous dreams sent by the angered spirit of Agamemnon, has for purposes of propitiation ordered maidens to offer libations at the King's tomb. Here Orestes makes himself known to his sister Electra and passes on to the palace, where he slays Aegisthus and Clytemnestra. The boy has religiously done his duty in avenging his father's blood, but in doing so he has slain his mother, and his conscience revolts at the terrible deed. His remorse is visualized by Aeschylus in a band of Furies. As these hell-hounds beset him the youth strives 'hard to tell his story ere his reason goes.' As he is driven from the stage the chorus sums up the cause of all this woe.

> Blown hath now the third harsh tempest,
> O'er the proud Atridian palace,
>   Floods of family woe!
> First thy damned feast, Thyestes,
> On thy children's flesh abhorrent;
> Then the kingly man's prostration,
> And thy warlike pride, Achaia,

73

> Butchered in a bath;
> Now he, too, our greeted Saviour
> Red with this new woe! —
> When shall Fate's stern work be ended,
> When shall cease the boistrous vengeance,
> Hushed in slumbers low?

In the *Eumenides*, the concluding part of the triology, the scene opens with Orestes clinging to the navel-stone in the temple of Apollo at Delphi, and the Furies asleep under the influence of the holy place. The god appears and, promising to support Orestes, directs him to go to Athens, where his case will be considered by just judges. In the temple of Pallas the youth is tried before a jury of Areopagites, Athene herself casting the deciding pebble in favor of acquittal. Thus the ancient curse was stayed when it fell upon a righteous man, and judicial process took the place of blood revenge. Orestes' vindication is based upon his rectitude, his obedience to the divine commands, his sufferings and lustrations. With the reign of law the vindictive Furies become the Eumenides, gracious ones, for conscience is friendly when men are obedient to the higher order.

I think Aeschylus chose this legend of the house of Atreus primarily to win the Athenians from the practice of blood revenge. Among primitive peoples, who made the family and not the individual the social unit, it was a religious duty for the next of kin to avenge murder. The injunction 'an eye for an eye and a tooth for a tooth' was recognized both in the Old Testament and in Homer. Unhappily, even among us, such feuds run down through generations. The poet reprobates this practice and advocates trial by jury as a more rational way to justice. He represents Athene, the Divine Wisdom, as presiding over the processes of law. Enlightened public opinion is a better method of settling disputes than individual revenge.

But the sources of power in the drama are far deeper than the wisdom of this civic instruction. Aeschylus, with all his stormy strength, was a man of tender heart, and the sufferings of the world weighed heavily upon him. Like the prophets, he asked for the cause of all this sorrow, and his reply was instant: it flows from human sin. He believed with his people that the origin of sin was some deed of insolent pride, and the horror of sin is that it sends its influences down through the family and out into devastating circles of injury to society. It is visited upon the children to the third and fourth generation, and demands an answering expiation.

He believed in the necessity of expiation with all his heart because of his keen sense of the majesty of the moral law and the certainty of its penalties. Only fools make a mock of sin; superior minds know its tragic nature. To him every sin grew out of some previous sin, and then became the fertile mother of other sins. There was a popular notion that the gods sent disasters because they were envious of the prosperity of men. Aeschylus declared that not the envy of heaven, but sin, is the cause of woe, and the cause of sin is pride.

> ... I know
> That impious deeds conspire
> To beget an offspring of impious deeds.

75

The Great Poets and the Meaning of Life

But whoso is just, though his wealth like a river
Flow down, shall be scathless, his house shall rejoice
In an offspring of beauty forever.

The chief reason why Aeschylus selected this particular legend was that it vividly set forth these three aspects of the nature of sin which he would enforce; its origin in pride or self-assertion, its fecundity in producing other evils, its inevitable retributions. These aspects he reveals through the clear statements of the chorus and in the development of the plot. According to tradition the curse resting upon the house of Atreus began with Tantalus, who in swollen pride disclosed the secrets of the gods and was sent to the labors of Tartarus. Pelops, his son, treacherously threw Myrtilus into the sea, who, drowning, cursed the house of Pelops. The crime of Atreus, son of Pelops, drew an added curse from his brother Thyestes. Thus the sin of Agamemnon, derived from the evil of his fathers, sent its entail of horror upon his children.

But Agamemnon is not an innocent victim of the family curse. The poet is at pains to show that by his own insolent pride he brought the evil of his house upon himself. His own free act involved him in the toils. His arrogant self-assertion is shown in the following experience. As the Greeks were starting on their expedition to Troy two eagles tore to pieces an exhausted hare bearing unborn young. The priest thus reads the omen: If Agamemnon and his brother go against Troy, they will destroy the city, but in doing so they will be guilty of monstrous vengeance, growing out of their uncontrolled love of glory. The cyclone of destruction will not be

76

justice, but excess of wrath, which the gods abhor. The joy of victory will be 'dashed not lightly with black bane,' and Fury will call to Fury.

Agamemnon accepts the omen and decides to proceed. His presumptuous pride awakens the divine anger. To satisfy this he sacrifices his daughter Iphigenia. As a king he has done his duty, even at woeful cost to himself. In doing so he has wronged the family and the home; he has let loose another evil which cries for recompense. Consequently on his return from the war his wife slays him in his bath. The blood of the innocent daughter has been avenged. With this retribution visited upon Agamemnon, the first play of the trilogy ends. Pride has been rebuked, and there has been blood for blood and blow for blow.

If sin originates in unwarranted assertion of self, its fertility is seen in the horrid brood of sorrows it produces. Troy is utterly wiped out and Greeks unnumbered are sent to gloomy Hades as a result of the commander's pride. He thought he was doing his patriotic duty in sacrificing his daughter, but in atoning for one wrong he perpetrates another which gives birth to subsequent bloodshed.

We of today are apt to think that sin is measured by the intention of the perpetrator. Not so the ancients. With them sin was gauged by its consequences, by the evil it sets in motion. No other book in literature puts so powerfully the horror and the closely linked woe of sin as this trilogy. Cassandra smelling the blood that stained the royal house and shrinking in terror from the doomed walls is one of the most overwhelming scenes ever put upon the stage. Clytemnestra exulting over a husband murdered is fearfully magnificent.

Fertile in disaster, sin invites inevitable retribution. In its beginning the evil deed may seem a trivial thing, but 'by their memories the gods are known,' and it is a divine decree that sin must be expiated. At first the lust of Paris appeared to be a soft infirmity,

> The gods are just and little caring
> So one hath said to mark the daring.

But Zeus, the protector of the wronged host's sacred right, was not forgetful, and the gentle grace of Helen proved the city's curse. The bow of Zeus was bent

> ... not before
> The fate-predestined hour, and not
> Beyond the stars with idle aim.

Every sin has its requital:

> 'Tis robber robbed, and slayer slain, for though
> Oft-times it lag, with measured blow for blow
> Vengeance prevaileth
> While great Jove lives. Who breaks the close-linked woe
> Which heaven entaileth?

Agamemnon has paid for Iphigenia's blood with his own. When Clytemnestra avenged her daughter by killing Agamemnon the family wronged the State, and this fresh wrong calls for atonement. In the Choephorae we read:

> Firm is the base of Justice, Fate
> With whetted knife doth eager wait
> At hoary Murder's door;

> The Fury, with dark bosomed ire,
> Doth send the son a mission dire,
>   To clear the parent's score.
>
> .   .   .   .
>
> Wont hath been, and shall be ever,
> That when purple gouts bedash
> The guilty ground, then BLOOD DOTH BLOOD
> DEMAND AND BLOOD FOR BLOOD SHALL FLOW.
> Fury to Havoc cries, and Havoc
> The tainted track of blood pursuing,
>   From age to age works woe.

Orestes must avenge his father's death by slaying his mother. This he does at the command of Apollo. But the dreadful deed arouses the Furies, who set upon him. In righting a wrong he has started a fresh evil. No wonder the chorus exclaims in the closing lines:

> Red with this new woe
> When shall Fate's stern work be ended,
> When shall cease the boistrous vengeance,
> Hushed in slumbers now?

For three generations and more evil has met its due recompense, yet each expiation set in motion a new stream of suffering. How break the chain and at last bring peace? In the *Eumenides* Aeschylus shows that reconciliation comes when a good man takes the curse upon himself, the gods temper justice with mercy, and public law takes the place of blood revenge.

Aeschylus put such tremendous stress upon punishment and expiation because he believed profoundly in the moral structure of the universe. God is righteous and will by no means clear the guilty. His conviction grew out of his own rugged conscience and the marvelous experiences of his

nation. A little people had miraculously been delivered
from destruction at the hands of the mightiest dynasty of
the world. The defeat of Persia indicated that the Supreme
was not on the side of the heaviest battalions, but was the
protector of the weak. He was righteous as well as mighty.
As a dramatist the poet saw in the legends of his people a
revelation of the way the Most High acts in human affairs.
I say the Most High, for the tendency of his mind was
strongly toward monotheism. The following is from a
fragment which has survived from a lost play:

> The air is Zeus, Zeus earth, and Zeus the heaven,
> Zeus all that is, and that transcends them all.

This thought of one supreme and just governor of the
heavens and earth was his spiritual refuge. In *Agamemnon*
he asserts:

> Zeus, or what other name
> The god that reigns supreme delights to claim,
> Him I invoke; him of all powers that be,
> Alone I find,
> From the bootless load of doubt can free
> My laboring mind.

There follows a curious passage in which he seems to
affirm that the progress of man was due to the improvement in the character of the heavenly ruler:

> Who was so great of yore,
> With all defiant valor brimming o'er
> Is mute, and who came next by a stronger arm
> Thrice vanquished fell;
> But thou hymn victor Jove; so in thy heart
> His truth shall dwell.

Aeschylus: *His Genius and Spiritual Insights*

According to popular mythology the world had been ruled by two dynasties before Zeus won the throne: first Uranos, then Cronos, then Zeus. The idea inculcated by the mythological succession is that the reign of brute force both in heaven and earth has at last become an order of justice and mercy. The Greek mind was not unfamiliar with the idea that man had come up from a condition of brutality to a condition in which moral sanctions were controlling.

The test of a dramatist's power is not in the number of his quotable sentences, but in his mastery over his central idea; not in the episodes, but in the effect of the whole. In this respect Aeschylus has no superior in the realm of his art. The total impression upon the reader or hearer of his plays is the supremacy of the Moral Order. The judge of all the earth will do right. Sin has its sure retribution. But God is also merciful, for through suffering comes reconciliation. No Hebrew believed this more sincerely or proclaimed it more powerfully. The forms in which he clothed his thought are not native to our way of thinking, yet they express principles of perpetual validity. Sin, in every generation and philosophy, expresses itself as excessive egoism, or selfishness. It disturbs the natural order, and its consequences stream far and wide. What Aeschylus called the family curse, we in scarcely less ignorance denominate hereditary tendencies. Blood revenge grows out of a true instinct; sin must be atoned, for every evil we must pay. Expiation is a law written deep in every man's heart, in his institutions, in the universe itself. But, as the author indicates, there are better ways of restoring the moral balance than blood for blood and blow for blow.

Implications

There are a number of implications here that are interesting and noteworthy. This trilogy reminds us that the tragedy of history is not the clash of right and wrong, but the clash of right with right. At every stage of this story each side was in the right from its own standpoint. Agamemnon, the King, promotes the public cause by sacrificing his child, but in doing so he wrongs the family. This Clytemnestra avenges, but in so doing slays the King, and injures the State. The repercussions between right and right cease when the burden falls upon one who represents both the State and the family, the Prince, who is righteous. He receives the conflict into his own breast and reconciles them because of his integrity. This idea of a righteous mediator, representative of both parties, reconciling them by his own sufferings has been prominent in religious thought ever since Job cried out for a daysman. Anselm expounded it in *Cur Deus Homo*, and for a thousand years it profoundly influenced theology.

It is to be noted also that in reconciliation the divine government suffers no dispraise. The Furies are honored and are seen to be, after all, Eumenides, gracious goddesses. For when personal vengeance gives place to public justice, and hate to mercy, then the moral law is seen to be friendly to man.

Aeschylus' mind was possessed of another truth of prodigious moment, namely, that wisdom is born of suffering, that out of evil good comes. The meaning of suffering in a just universe has been a problem engaging the profoundest minds since history began. Aeschylus makes it the central thought of the trilogy of which only *Prometheus Bound* remains to us. He presents the pathetic figure of Io, wronged by Zeus, driven over the earth by a gadfly, watched by Argos of a hundred eyes. He shows us Prometheus, the sincere friend of man, tortured for some thirty thousand years because of his good deeds. In the drama we are made to see the violent antagonism between human aspirations and the will of Heaven, but to our great loss the measure and method of the reconciliation have not been preserved. That the author does work out a solution is indicated by the strange prophecy, written some five hundred years before Calvary, that by the vicarious intervention of a god who would take upon himself the sufferings of the victim, Prometheus would be released. Hermes, in rebuking the Titan for his impotent rage against Zeus, after foretelling new tortures declares:

> Do not look
> For any end moreover to this curse,
> Or ere some god appear to accept thy pangs
> On his own head vicarious, and descend
> With unreluctant steps the darks of hell
> And gloomy abysses around Tartarus.

Such evidence as we have indicates that Zeus and Prometheus were reconciled because each became wise through suffering, and even Io's brutal wrongs wrought out at last perfect peace. In *Agamemnon*, written later, Aeschylus distinctly declares that suffering is the chosen instrument used by Zeus to teach men wisdom:

> For Jove doth teach men wisdom, sternly wins
> To virtue by the tutoring of their sins.

83

And further on:

> Justice doth wait to teach
> Wisdom by suffering.

Professor Gilbert Murray says that 'Ionia never gave us this thought. It is peculiarly the gift of Athens.' But surely the same question was asked and explicitly answered in Job, in Isaiah, fifty-third chapter, and in many of the Psalms. And the Church has proclaimed for two thousand years that the Captain of Salvation was made perfect through suffering.

Conclusion

One who dwells with Aeschylus for a length of time is surely lifted into the realms of power and has his heart purged by elevated feelings. In sheer sublimity and elemental energy he looms a Titan among other poets. The fire of war is in his blood and it flames in his verses, yet his passion is controlled by a steady moral purpose. Although he dealt with primitive ideas, the dramatist saw in them symbols of fundamental principles which he enforced with all his magnificent energy. No man was ever more conscious that the universe in which we are living is a moral universe. Every evil is begotten of evil and produces a brood of other evils. Every wrong is the offspring of some wrong of other days. In what the populace called the family curse, he saw the workings of the ancient law which cannot be repealed: the sins of the fathers are visited upon the children unto the third and fourth generation.

To Aeschylus the moral order is attested by two unimpeachable witnesses; the Law of Heredity and the Law of Expiation. Sin is not a negligible thing; its consequences go down through the generations, sons suffer for their parents' folly. Sins also crash through the social order and set man against man, institution against institution, and there can be no reconciliation until there has been an atonement. The cause of evil is sin, sin in some form of excess, which thus violates what to a Greek was the fundamental law of life, 'nothing too much.' This terrible austerity of the moral order is mitigated by three important facts.

First, man is dowered with the gift of free will. He is not the helpless victim of an inexorable fate. Only by some act of his own does he link himself with the curse upon his house. If his will is bent on righteousness then the gods are on his side. His virtue makes him a moral victor. The upright will of Orestes is triumphant over the tainted blood that flows in his veins from both sides of his house. 'Nowhere,' writes Professor Butcher, 'is man's essential spiritual freedom more vigorously asserted than in Aeschylus.'

The second fact is that the suffering of the innocent is expiatory. In this Aeschylus glimpses the power which Isaiah discloses in that profound fifty-third chapter. Orestes checks the clash between the family and the State because, as prince and son, he is the representative of both parties, and being a righteous man, obedient to the gods, the Furies become the Eumenides. By the afflictions of the righteous, reconciliation is won. Then there is that strange intuition that a god must descend into Tartarus to release Prometheus.

The third fact which deeply impressed the poet was that through suffering comes wisdom. No more than others could he solve the problem of human suffering, but he found a partial solution and great consolation in the thought that through sad experiences wisdom is born.

As Aeschylus brooded upon the confused scene of humanity, bewildered, tortured, clashing in the darkness, he saw clearly the law of retribution. Beyond this he saw help from the Unseen. The gods (Athene and Apollo), strengthening the moral will of the righteous sufferer, bring reconciliation and peace at last.

LUCRETIUS: *A Materialistic Philosophy Becomes Noble Poetry*

In the. great succession of poets of epic grandeur Rome produced but two, Lucretius and Virgil, whom we shall now study.

The Man

Unlike most of the Roman writers, Lucretius gives us no hint, in the only work which has come down to us, *De Rerum Natura*, of his position or his experience. Cicero, who was about eight years his senior and read the poem, which the author left unfinished, gives us no information concerning him. Some four hundred years after Lucretius, Jerome, in short accounts of distinguished men which were based upon information drawn from a lost work of Suetonius, records under the year 94 B.C., *Titus Lucretius poeta nascitur.* Jerome further states that a love philtre had made the poet mad, but during his sane intervals he had written several books which Cicero corrected, and that he died of his own hand in the forty-fourth year of his age. As Suetonius wrote some two centuries after

87

Lucretius, the story of the love philtre is supposed to be a legend; and as Jerome in his summaries was often careless in his dates, authorities incline to put the birth of the poet about the year 98 B.C. They also accept the statement of Donatus in his life of Virgil that Lucretius died on the same day that Virgil assumed the *toga virilis*, October 15, 55 B.C. This would agree with the statement that he died in his forty-fourth year. That he may have had a period of mental derangement is not incredible when we consider the intensity and susceptibility of his temperament as revealed in his work. That his great poem was left unfinished, like Virgil's *Aeneid*, is probable, judging from its disjointed structure and its many repetitions. Such evidence as we can derive from his writings indicates that he belonged to the Roman aristocracy and possessed sufficient wealth to live in studious leisure. If so, he is the only poet of the pure Roman stock to attain the first rank. As he was about two years younger than Julius Caesar and died when Caesar was invading Britain, we know that his life was passed in a period of upheaval and confusion; a time when the stable order of society was torn asunder by the insatiable greed and towering ambitions of great commanders.

Lucretius was an ardent disciple of Epicurus, in whose philosophy he believed he had found a way of life that would free men from the excesses of personal ambition, and restore to them serenity and inward strength in those distracting times. His was the faith and zeal of an earnest moral teacher, but his also was the joy and pride of a poet. 'A great hope of praise,' he writes, 'has pricked my heart with a sharpened goad, and also has inspired my breast with sweet love of the Muses.' Quickened by this love he traverses paths untrodden by men and drinks of springs before untouched. He is confident that he will succeed in his high endeavor, 'first, because I am a teacher of great themes, intent to free the mind from close drawn bonds of superstition; next, because on a dark theme I pen so lucid verses, shedding over all the charm of poetry.' He puts his philosophy in hexameters to render it acceptable, 'as doctors, when their purpose is to give to children nauseous wormwood, first anoint the rim about with honey's sweet and golden juice.'

The Poem

The character of the monumental work of Lucretius is sufficiently indicated by its title, *De Rerum Natura* ('Concerning the Nature of Things'). It is a philosophy of materialism expressed in noble hexameter verse, and is one of the supreme efforts of the ancient mind to account for Nature and her processes and man and his experiences. It was the conviction of Lucretius that the happiness and dignity of life depend upon one's freedom from superstition. In his opinion, dread of the capricious gods and fear of the life after death were among the chief evils afflicting humanity. He would persuade men that the gods never interfere with human concerns, that Nature is not controlled by fickle impulse, but is orderly and wonderful, as, like Penelope, she weaves and unweaves her web. Death as well as life is part of the eternal process, and should be accepted with tranquil mind. That men may live simply, more courageously, less passionately, he would make them realize how ephemeral are all human values.

The poem is of peculiar interest today, for it treats of the subjects which most engage this scientific age — the evolution of the universe, the nature of the atom, the origin of man, the causes of his customs and his progress.

> It still remains [writes one of his best interpreters] an astonishing fact that many of the most important physical discoveries of modern times are hinted at or even expressly stated by Lucretius. The general outlines of the atomic doctrine have long been accepted as in the main true, in all important features it is superior to any other physical theory of the universe which existed up to the seventeenth century. In his theory of light Lucretius was in advance of Newton. In his theory of chemical affinities (for he describes the thing though the nomenclature was unknown to him) he was in advance of Lavoisier. In his theory of the ultimate constitution of the atom he is in striking agreement with the views of the ablest living physicists.[1]

Lucretius was born too soon to work according to the scientific method, but he possessed imaginative insight to an extraordinary degree, so that he takes the reader with him into Nature's workshop and reveals many of her methods. The substance of his materialistic philosophy was not original with him. He inherited it from Democritus through Epicurus. But he was its ablest advocate. His peculiar contribution was his keen observation of the ways of nature, his comprehensive grasp of facts, his powerful assembling of evidence, and, above all, his poetic

[1] Mackail, J. W., *Latin Literature*, p. 44.

imagination, which easily rises from details to a contemplation of the cosmos, making the reader feel its unity, its amazing grandeur, to his soul's elation.

The evidence of his extraordinary genius is seen in the fact that he could soar so high carrying so heavy a load. He only among poets has been able out of materials and methods of physical science to make a great poem, and he has done this because the white heat of his passion for truth has suffused his unpromising material with its own power. His sense of the interrelationship of all things, and his sublime confidence in the mind's power to know, is memorably expressed in the closing lines of the first book:

> One thing after another will grow clear, and dark night shall not rob you of the road and keep you from surveying the utmost ends of nature; in such wise things will light the torch for other things.[1]

Here we see one of the strongest minds of antiquity in the first dawn of science, striving to answer the problem of man and his universe, not by myths, but by searching for the causes of phenomena, and uttering his thought in the noblest and most sonorous lines to be found in a language which above all others is noble and sonorous.

The poem is composed of six books. In the first two the author affirms that the atoms and space are ultimate realities. The atoms are indestructible, infinite in number, limited in variety, different in shape, and in constant motion. Their fortuitous combinations form the present

[1] Munro's translation.

order, which will dissolve, and new combinations, new worlds, new institutions, new men will be formed. In such a system there is no room for caprice or Providence.

> For blindly, blindly, and without design,
>   Did these first atoms their first meetings try.
> No ordering thought was there, no will divine
>   To guide them; but through infinite time gone by
> Tossed and tormented they essayed to join,
>   And clashed through the void space tempestuously,
> Until at last that certain whirl began,
> Which slowly formed the earth and heaven and man.[1]

The third book shows that the soul, the vital principle, perishes with the body. This is central in his thought: 'Why dost thou not retire like a banqueter filled with life, and calmly, O fool, take thy peaceful sleep?' Book Four treats of dreams and visions as related to a belief in life after death. Book Five shows how the heavens, the earth, and man came into existence without divine initiative, and the last book explains the phenomena — such as earthquakes and thunder — which by the superstitious are attributed to the wrath of the gods.

In Lucretius we have the profoundest mind of the Latin race which has applied itself to poetic expression. His task was enormous. In an undeveloped language, having few words for abstract thought, he undertook to expound a system of philosophy, and as though this were not difficult enough, he subdued philosophy to the demands of verse. So intensely in earnest was he to present the whole truth that his lines are often overweighted with thought and the poetry stiffens into prose. Yet, lying like fertile valleys

[1] Translated by W. H. Mallock.

amid rugged mountains, there is true poetry, such as his preludes and his tribute to Epicurus.

> When human life, a shame to human eyes,
>   Lay sprawling in the mire in foul estate,
> A cowering thing without the strength to rise,
>   Held down by fell Religion's heavy weight —
> Religion scowling downward from the skies,
>   With hideous head, and vigilant eyes of hate —
> First did a man of Greece presume to raise,
> His brows, and give the monster gaze for gaze.
>
> Him not the tales of all the gods in heaven,
>   Nor heaven's lightnings, nor the menacing roar
> Of thunder daunted. He was only driven,
>   By these vain vauntings, to desire the more
> To burst through Nature's gates, and rive the unriven
>   Bars. And he gained the day; and, conqueror,
> His spirit broke beyond our world, and past
> Its flaming walls, and fathomed all the vast.[1]

With him the poetry appears to be in the object rather than in the singer. His imagination is not an instrument for creating a golden atmosphere which transforms the ugly features of reality; it is a faculty by which he apprehends the harmony abiding in the nature of things. He describes his facts vividly, masses them in formidable groups, and uses only those poetical allusions which grow out of his subject and his own experience. Through all the poem from beginning to end sounds the note of perfect sincerity.

The Poet's Cosmic Vision

It is the tendency of polytheism to fix attention on what is separate and distinct; it is engaged with the various

[1] Mallock's translation.

aspects of life; yet, as we have seen, both Homer and Aeschylus, especially the latter, had glimpses of a controlling unity. But this thought was in the background. With Lucretius, however, the focus of his attention was the universe, the Whole in which all things played their part and found their meaning. After all, his predecessors, great poets though they were, lived in a very constricted scheme of things. Lucretius was the first poet of the western world to set his thought to the scale of infinity. His was a cosmic consciousness in which the Many formed the One, and the majesty of the vision was a radical spiritual experience in its elevating and cleansing power. He was also the first of the poets to affirm a universe governed by law; and this at a time when the common mind was controlled by superstitious fears and thought of the world as managed by many unpredictable forces and unreliable gods. For one to hold centrally in his thought a conception of an orderly universe, in which one found salvation by ascertaining the causes of events and obeying the sure workings of nature, rather than by magic and ceremonial, was a notable achievement. Mr. Santayana, in his stimulating study of the poet, declares that 'a naturalistic conception of things is a great work of the imagination — greater, I think, than any dramatic or moral mythology; it is a conception fit to inspire great poetry, and in the end, perhaps, it will prove the only conception able to inspire it.'[1]

The grandeur of this high fantasy is beyond question. It is composed of three elements. First, Infinite Space,

[1] *Three Philosophical Poets*, p. 21.

in which the lightning, rushing on forever in its vast stretches, would never find the boundary; in which there is no rim where one may stand and be unable to cast a javelin further; secondly, Atoms, indestructible, many-shaped, limited in variety but unlimited in number; thirdly, Motion. The atoms move ceaselessly with inconceivable rapidity, integrating and disintegrating in constant flux, an endless stream, flowing forever through the eternal Void. Out of this combination of Void, Matter, and Motion have heaven and earth and all that is therein been born. These appear for a moment of time and then are dissolved into their elements, which are organized again in different shapes. Then why should we fear death? It is part of the natural order. Where we are death is not, and where death is we are not. The Unconscious Swirl moves on forever unmindful of its unrestingness. It neither hates nor loves us, it knows us not. Men have their brief moments of sensuous life and then return to their primal elements. What was earth goes back to the dust to be refashioned in other forms, and the soul, that finer form of matter, which came from the 'ether coasts,' goes back to the sky.

It is a tremendous picture. No one can let his thoughts range through time and space and human experience without ennobling his imagination and cleansing his spirit, at least for the moment, from all pettiness. This conception of the vastness and ordered wholeness of a universe is certainly a nobler creation of the imagination than the brilliant mythology crowded with the Olympians. It is inferior only to that other vision — the loftiest of which the human imagination is capable — which includes all that the materialist sees, plus Something, which we believe is not entirely alien to us, and which we interpret through the highest symbols our minds can form — Spirit, Light, Purpose, Love. When we apply these words to the Eternal we are aware how man-made and imperfect they are, but they are the best symbols we have. Certainly he is not less than our highest conceptions, and we believe he is infinitely above them. This pervading God we think of as guiding creation to a goal not unworthy of the cost of the process. He means intensely and he means good.

The effect of the philosophy of materialism as taught by Lucretius depends upon the nature and condition of the one receiving it. To many it means only release from restraint and the unleashing of the passions: 'Let us eat, drink and be merry, for tomorrow we die.' To the ordinary upright citizen it would seem to be lacking in all that makes the heart element in religion. It offers no place for prayer, and all the realms of help are empty. To Lucretius himself it came as to one who had found great treasure. It liberated him from fear of death, the dread of fickle gods, the mistakes of superstition. His vision of the vastness and fidelity of the universe stirred within him noble and purifying emotions. It dowered him with that high gift we call 'cosmic enthusiasm.' It kindled his mind to wonder, a wonder which led to rapture, a rapture which burst into noble poetry.

His belief profoundly influenced his attitude toward life. By it he arrived at a condition which is fundamental in all religion: He accepted the universe, and in the surrender he found peace of mind. By acquiescence he became free. By working with nature he was conscious of a certain mastery over nature. His mood became like that of his master, Epicurus, who, passing far beyond the flaming walls of the world, 'traversed throughout in mind and spirit the immeasurable universe, whence he returns a conqueror to tell us what can, what cannot come into being — on what principle each has its powers defined, its deep-set boundary mark.' [1] It tended to cultivate another most important virtue — that of detachment. Ambitions and troubles lose their insistency when one remembers the trampling of the ages and the limitless abysses of space. The view from these high seats teaches one wisdom. From them 'you may look down upon others and see them wandering all abroad and going astray in their search for the path of life, see the contest among them of intellect, the rivalry of birth, the striving night and day with surpassing effort to struggle to the summit of power and be masters of the world. O miserable minds of men! O blinded breasts!' [2]

And in another place he declares that there are elevations in the lofty mountains from which the restless men on the plain appear to be still, and their glitter a quiet gleam.

In the turmoil of militant Rome, he only was serene. One who in thought habitually measures the things and experiences of life against the Timeless and the Infinite is contented with a very little, and these the simple and common things. He does not lust for power, or place, or

[1] Munro's translation, 1:62 ff.   [2] *Ibid.*, 2:8-13.

pleasure; rather he seeks to master his own passions and to be conqueror of himself. If he suffers, he neither rails at Fate, nor prays to the unreplying gods; he seeks to find out the causes of his woe and remove them.

A well thought out philosophy of materialism has value for its insistence on the universal reign of law. Every effect has its cause; the 'way of wisdom' is to learn the sure ways of nature and obey them. This is the path of progress. That he is living in a dependable world is one of the most comforting and beneficent beliefs man has yet achieved. This Lucretius believed with all the energy of his nature. To drive the idea of caprice from the world was his passion. To have lifted up in an age of superstition and terror the idea of unvarying law was a service of great moment.

In a true sense he had the spirit of high religion. His mind was centered on the Everlasting, the Infinite, and this lifted him out of a destructive selfishness. He accepted the universe in a humble spirit, and his dominant enthusiasms were a passion for truth and a passion for service. One feels in him the note of moral greatness, a hatred of hypocrisy, an intellectual integrity, a noble self-reliance which effect the reader for good. The literature of revolt has produced no nobler spirit. He faced the universe and was unafraid.

The materialistic philosophy doubtless contains a valid aspect of reality, but it is hopelessly simple. It leaves out too much which the long experience of the world shows to be of greatest value and highest probability. Nevertheless it goes far and has been welcomed by some of the noblest minds of the race. Yet too often it is abused by men of less noble character as an excuse for unrestrained impulse.

This is Lucretius' contribution to the life of the spirit. In a world where men are prone to superstition, magic, pride, and chaos he erected a powerful vision of an orderly universe in which men lighten their burdens by studying the natural sources of evil, and find liberty, peace, and power by working in harmony with the Nature of Things. He was not the first to think these thoughts, but he was the first to turn a great philosophy into an immortal song.

The Realms of Help

Having indicated the poet's chief contribution to the higher life of humanity, it remains to point out another resource of spiritual refreshment of which he availed himself, apart from his sense of the orderly processes of nature. Like all other mortals, he needed help, and like them he turned to the Unseen, and there he found what he craved. As he walked the streets of Rome, or entered the silent temples, the beauty of the statues of the gods cast their spell upon him. They spoke to him of peace, of divine calm, of ideal beauty. As he contemplated them he experienced unwonted spiritual elation and into his heart came mysterious strength. His explanation of this inner quietness and reinforcement is exceedingly interesting.

He believed with his master, Epicurus, that the gods exist. They are not the determiners of human destiny, nor the controllers of the forces of nature; neither are they the irresponsible and immoral beings of popular mythology.

They are the products of the order of nature, of a higher species than men, and are blessed with endless life, perpetual joy, and perfect righteousness.

They dwell in the lucid interspaces of the worlds, so effectively described by Tennyson's transcription of the words of Lucretius;

> Where never creeps a cloud, or moves a wind,
> Nor ever falls the least white star of snow,
> Nor ever lowest roll of thunder moans,
> Nor sound of human sorrow mounts to mar
> Their sacred everlasting calm....

The gods, in his thought, were perfect beings, living in fullness of joy in a flawless environment. Their bodies were indeed physical, but the atoms composing them were so fine that they escaped mortal touch or sight. Abiding in the upper ether, and untroubled by human sorrow, they still helped. From their radiant bodies issued forth a filmy substance, tenuous and vitalizing, which entered the open mind of the devout worshiper as a healing and enlightening energy. The gods possessed everlastingly what mortals most desire, and their glory and power flowed from them. Being a convinced Epicurean, the poet could adore and pray, and his prayers were answered. Calmness and strength came into his surrendered mind. The gods might be unaware of their worshiper, but their light and power entered for healing into the mortal attuned to their high ministry.

So did this Roman poet, through the never-changing human process of surrender, adoration, and prayer to the highest perfection he knew, open the gates of his being to the realms of help.

VIRGIL: *Who Placed an Ideal Before Imperial Rome*

ON THE day Lucretius died, a youth who was to become a greater poet, but not a greater man, assumed the *toga virilis*. The date was the fifteenth of October, 55 B.C.; the youth was Publius Vergilius Maro.

The younger poet was far more fortunate than his predecessor in the materials of his art which he inherited, and in the times in which he lived. The virile tongue of Latium, at first only fitted for war and commerce, had for two centuries been subject to the labor of poets and orators, until it had developed a precision, a flexibility in the expression of subtle thought, a grace of phrase, which made it capable of the highest literary use. 'There is for literature, a moment, slow to come and swift to pass, when the language, polished and made pliant by use, lends itself to the most vivid and most exact expression of conceptions, which have themselves been developed by the long labor of genius. It was thus with Latin literature... when Virgil and Horace came to gather the fruits of poetry, mature at last.' [1]

[1] Patin, *La Poésie latine*; quoted by Glover, *Virgil*, p. 58.

The period in which the poet lived was favorable to the production of refined literary art. Lucretius had toiled in a time of intense civil commotion; the whole world was in turmoil. Virgil learned hatred of war and pity for suffering during the civic upheavals of his youth, but his genius ripened in one of the world's greatest epochs of peace and prosperity. The times were propitious to dream of the return of the Golden Age, to celebrate the arts of husbandry and the charms of Italy, to recall the strange ways by which the gods had directed the Roman people in their astonishing career of conquest. Moreover Virgil became an intimate friend of Augustus, and thus was at the center where all influences converged. Here his exquisitely sensitive nature discerned all the deeper currents of this extraordinary age. These he interpreted, revealing to Rome her noblest mood, and to the world the loftiest spiritual aspirations of the Empire. Like Homer and Dante, Virgil stood at one of the great divides of history, on a distinct line marking the waning of an old order and the glorious appearance of a new.

Events of Virgil's Life

Publius Vergilius [1] Maro was born October 15, in the year 70 B.C., near Mantua, during the consulate of Pompey and Crassus. His father was a freeholder who tilled his own soil and was eager to give his children the largest oppor-

---

[1] In the oldest manuscripts the name of the poet is spelled with *e*; but from the fifth century A.D. the name has established itself in European literature as Virgil.

tunities for culture and position. The boy Virgil grew up with a deep love of country life and with an intimate knowledge of the ways of husbandry. 'He loved trees as Homer did the sea,' and something of the manner of a rustic clung to him throughout his life. After studying in Cremona and Milan he went to Rome to be trained in rhetoric, probably in deference to his father's ambition that he become an advocate. The youth had little taste for this career or for its preparatory studies. The words of the rhetoricians were to him 'empty color bottles,' 'tinkling cymbals,' and he turned with eagerness to study philosophy under Siro, the Epicurean, who had the divine gift of communicating to his hearers a strong love of philosophy, a love which continued with Virgil to the end. Perhaps this change was influenced by Lucretius' great poem, *De Rerum Natura*, which was published about the time Virgil went to Rome. We know that the spell of its thought and manner was felt profoundly by the younger poet.

Returning to his home, he seems to have lived a life of studious leisure, cultivating his mind and practicing his craft. After the battle of Philippi, the victors, Octavian and Antony, to compensate their soldiers, confiscated land in the territories which had taken the republican side. Among the estates thus seized was the one belonging to Virgil's father, and the family was driven out.

This misfortune seemed tragic at the time. To be an exile and impoverished cut deeply into the sensitive nature of the poet, but, as so often happens, things evil finally reveal a soul of goodness. Genius in a little experience apprehends much, and through the memory of his own sufferings there came into Virgil's poetry that note of pity which is so distinctive and engaging. This episode not only enriched his moral nature; it had a most favorable result upon his career, for in his efforts to regain his homestead he came to the notice of Octavian, who became his friend. The patronage of the head of the State gave him fortune, leisure, an attentive public; it also inspired and moulded his masterpiece.

It is supposed that the homestead was restored, but when Virgil went to take possession, the angry veteran who held it as a prize of war drove him off, and he plunged into the river to escape personal violence. Soon afterwards we find him again in Rome, a member of that brilliant circle of which Pollio, Maecenas, Horace, and Varius were members, and upon whom shone steadily the royal favor. It is said that Virgil was given a house in Rome, which he seldom used, and a villa near Naples. How abundant his revenues became is shown by the fact that when he died he left property equivalent to about five hundred thousand dollars of our money.

When he was about thirty-two years of age, he published a collection of poems, known as the *Eclogues*, the word meaning short, selected pieces. They had immediate and phenomenal success.

Some seven years later he published a maturer and more highly finished work, the *Georgics*. Both poets and critics consider the *Georgics*, in range of thought and sentiment, in mastery of material, in the music of its lines, in its sincerity and freedom, the best of Virgil's works. Soon after its completion the poet set himself seriously to the task of his epic. Ten years he was absorbed in the *Aeneid*, which he wrote for the most part in Naples and its vicinity.

In the year 19 B.C., for inspiration and change of scene he journeyed to Athens. Here he met the Emperor, who persuaded him to return to Italy. On a very hot day the two visited the ruins of Megara, where the poet contracted a fever which grew worse as he continued his journey, until on reaching Brundisium he was unable to proceed further and died, September 21, 19 B.C.

Although the *Aeneid* was completed, it had need of thorough revision. To this revision the poet had intended to give the next three years. So keen was his sense of the unfinished condition of the epic that he wished to burn it; then, as no one would bring the manuscript to him, he charged his executors to publish nothing which he had not already given to the world. But the Emperor prized the poem too highly to allow it to be lost, and ordered it published as Virgil had left it. The poet was buried at Naples and his tomb became a holy place.

Our purpose is to find the spiritual values of the works of Virgil; to ascertain, as far as possible, his attitude towards life and his judgment of it; what principles of action he assumed as valid; what were his aspirations and his constant faith; above all, what truth or ideal he has established as a permanent possession of mankind, what sentiment or emotion he has so shaped by his genius that it still bears his stamp.

THE ECLOGUES: *Their Spiritual Value*

The first writings important to our purpose are the *Eclogues*, published when the poet was thirty-two years of age, and written in the halcyon days when he was wandering in the realms of gold and cultivating his gift of song. Imitating the pastoral verses of Theocritus, he essayed to sing the beauties of Italy as the Greek had sung of the shepherds and fields of Sicily. Of the ten poems making this collection, the Fourth has achieved remarkable fame and is germane to our purpose.

It appears to have been written in the year 40 B.C., a time when there were hopeful signs that the world, exhausted by a hundred years of war, spoliation, and civic discord, would at last have peace. Antony and Octavian having signed a treaty of reconciliation, men hoped for a period of domestic tranquillity. Virgil especially experienced a sense of security under the extending power of Octavian, which inspired him to visualize a warless world and a lasting peace. Under the exaltation of this lofty vision the poet wrote these marvelous words;

> Now come the world's last days, the age foretold
> By Cumae's prophetess in sacred song.
> The vast world-process brings a new-born time.
> Once more the Virgin comes and Saturn's reign,
> Behold a heaven-born offspring earthward hies!
> Holy Lucina, lend thy light and aid
> The while this child is born before whose power
> The iron race of mortals shall away,
> And o'er this earth a golden people reign,
> For blest Apollo is at last their king.

Under thy fasces, Pollio, forth shall shine
This glory of our age; guided by thee
These potent times begin . . . [1]

The poem continues, predicting that this child shall live a life divine and rule over a warless world, the bountiful earth without labor shall bring forth abundant harvests, the sheep shall of the lion be unafraid, the oaks shall distill honey. When the child shall have attained full maturity commerce shall cease, for the fields shall produce an abundance for all, the very wool of the sheep shall be gorgeous with natural purple, and saffron, and vermilion. The poem closes with an exhortation to the divine child to receive the glory which awaits him.

Such predictions, coming from Rome's supreme poet a few years before the birth of Christ, were eagerly welcomed by the early Church as additional evidence of the supernatural mission and the universal rule of the Nazarene, and greatly enhanced the fame of Virgil. He was considered the 'prophet of the Gentiles,' a 'Christian without Christ,' and his tomb became a shrine for the devout. The Fourth Eclogue ranks in interest with the major prophecies of the race, making the author more than the chief poet of the Latins, even a spiritual authority throughout Europe, a witness to a religion of which he had never heard.

Much has been written concerning the identity of the divine babe. Some claim that the poet had in mind the son of that Pollio to whom the poem was dedicated; others that he was Marcellus, son of Octavia; others that he was

[1] T. C. Williams's translation.

the expected child of Scribonia, who was married that year to Augustus, and when the boy turned out to be a girl — the far from divine Julia — Virgil thought the words vague enough to remain unmodified.

The similarity of this prediction to Isaiah's prophecy of the Messianic Age and the coming king is very striking. Both speak of the Virgin, the miraculous child, the reign of righteousness, the lion and the lamb, the abundant fruitfulness of the peaceful earth. Was Virgil familiar with Isaiah, and did he borrow from him? We know that Isaiah's prophecies were accessible in the Septuagint to the Greek scholars of Alexandria, and it is not impossible that Virgil, an erudite student, and in his early days much influenced by Alexandrine literature, may have heard some echoes of the word of the poet of Judah. But this is certainly not a case of direct borrowing. The aspiration of a perfected world is universal, and has been voiced through the centuries by the poets. Saint Paul in the eighth chapter of Romans has a marvelous personification of Nature, groaning and travailing in pain, waiting for the coming of a diviner race which shall deliver her from bondage. But two thousand years before Saint Paul there came from Egypt a similar announcement of a better world under a divine ruler. Here are the words of Neferrohu, foretelling, in a time of painful disillusionment, the advent of a king who would redeem Egypt; 'The people of his time shall rejoice, the son of man shall make his name forever and ever.... Righteousness shall return to its place, unrighteousness shall be cast out.' [1] Such words are not the

[1] Breasted, J. H., *The Dawn of Conscience*, p. 102.

result of special enlightenment, but of confident hope.

Interesting as this eclogue is, and extensive as was its influence in the early days of the Church, it is, after all, a young poet's aspiration. Mr. Glover writes truly, 'It is as much a prayer as a prophecy.' Surely a description of a golden age which culminates in purple and saffron lambs indicates that the young man's prayer degenerated into fancy, quite different from the sustained passion for righteousness which distinguished the prophets of Israel.

Yet these verses do give us a glimpse into the soul of Virgil and reveal what he considered to be of supreme value. They show him to be a lover of peace, convinced that universal happiness comes only under a stable and just government. To him the hope of the world is not in the wisdom of the masses; it is in the insight and rectitude of great leaders who come at the appointed times, and they come because the supreme God is concerned for men and is working out his own purpose in the nation.

The strong sense of a Power not ourselves, working through nations and individuals for peace and righteousness, is a major religious insight; and the faith in progress and the hope for humanity which it brings are of fundamental importance in a judgment on the worth of life. The vision of a better world, to be accomplished through the providential ordering of events, became later a conviction and the structural idea of the *Aeneid*. The appearance in Rome amid the welter of its politics of this dominant thought of the Hebrew prophets is most worthy of note.

THE GEORGICS

The youthful poet might dream delightfully of a golden age and a perfect king, but the actual world in which he was living seemed fast degenerating. The population was leaving the farms and villages and crowding into the cities, where they became dependent on the charity of the State, the rich were indulging in ruinous luxury, the virtues which had made Rome great were disappearing. The government felt the necessity of turning the attention of the people to the advantages of country life that the primitive virtues might be revived and nourished. Moreover, the disbanded armies had been rewarded by gifts of land, and there was need to instruct the new farmers in the ways of husbandry, and to make them contented with their lot by teaching them to appreciate its pleasures and dignity. To inaugurate a 'back to the farm' movement, Maecenas brought pressure to bear on Virgil to use his gifts to turn the attention of the public to the simple joys and the sane satisfactions of the country.

The task was a congenial one for a poet who loved the country and understood work on the farm. Retiring to his home in Campania, which had been given him in compensation for the one he had lost, Virgil spent seven years in composing the *Georgics* — four poems celebrating the arts of husbandry, the wine and trees of Italy, the breeding and care of sheep and goats, the culture of bees and the wonder of their communal life. He not only wrote of these things poetically, he gave detailed and wise instructions about managing the farm so as to make it most profitable.

When the poems were finished, the author in four successive days read them to Augustus, Maecenas relieving the poet when his voice was weary. The *Georgics* were published in the year 29 B.C., when Virgil was in his forty-first year, and established his reputation immediately as one of the foremost of Latin poets.

To look for important religious values in bucolic propaganda seems on first thought to be futile; on the contrary, the poems are rich in the material which makes for the abundant life. Virgil was a man of broad sympathies, and entered into the sufferings of men and even of animals most naturally. Therefore through the *Georgics* there is a vein of that fine religious sentiment which is native to the understanding heart. A lover of nature, he felt deeply her beauty, and like Wordsworth had a sense of something still more deeply interfused, a spiritual presence which disturbed him with the joy of elevated thoughts, and he exhorts all husbandmen to work in the consciousness of the divine presence and to keep in right relations with the higher Power. Warde Fowler affirms that Virgil 'more warmly and sympathetically than any other Latin author gives expression to the best religious feeling of the Roman mind.'

Virgil succeeds in presenting rural life lighted by the golden atmosphere of the ideal. What most men need to give zest to existence is not a new occupation or changed conditions; it is the new spirit which comes from beholding the old tasks glorified by an ideal. The drudgery of the farm, touched by the magic of the poet's imagination, becomes fascinating. He shows the farmer how to hitch

his plow to a star, he makes him feel the beauty and wonder of the world, and teaches him that work is a gospel.
His life may be hard, but Jove intended it to be hard, for
only through labor does one achieve blessedness, and, like
the bee, render due service to the whole.

Moreover, we find revealed to the husbandman a
practical way of attaining those supreme values which
have been the aspiration of mankind in all centuries and
all countries. Peace, personal liberty, happiness, for these
the generations of men have toiled, yet they are far from
being established in the world of affairs. Religion prospers in so far as it gives these to the individual as an immediate personal experience. The poet points out how
favorable are the conditions of a farmer's life to the possession of these highest values. Independent, as few men
are, he works in harmony with nature and thus finds
peace; he has a sense that life is worth while because it is
of service; joy comes through understanding and appreci-
ating the beauty and the wonder of nature. 'Happy is he
who knows the rural gods.'

Virgil was not so profound a thinker as Lucretius, but
he was a man of pitying sympathies, and in the *Georgics*
he has set forth an ideal of a life free, independent, at
peace with itself, because in harmony with nature and the
divine purpose. It is powerful preaching according to the
methods of art. It is the most substantial and artistically
perfect of all those books on the delights of the farmer's
life, which, from time to time, are written by poetic souls
in crowded cities as they meditate upon their youth and
the peace of the hills.

THE AENEID

Upon the completion of the *Georgics*, Virgil set himself earnestly to produce the epic poem which was to be his chief title to fame. He had worked successfully with the lyric style in the *Eclogues*; he had made a still greater success with didactic poetry in the *Georgics*; now, in the maturity of his powers, he was to test his genius in the bolder venture of the epic.

He wrote under many motives. As a poet he was eager to rival the great Homer; he would prove that Roman genius was in no way inferior to the Greek, and he would celebrate the majesty of Rome and of Augustus. But deeper than these, and more determinative of the structure and development of his poem, was his purpose to reveal to the Romans their God-given destiny and elevate their characters to the level of their divine mission. He felt deeply that the sovereign position of the Roman people and the throne of Augustus were not events resting on accidental success; they were decreed in heaven; they were the result of a providential ordering of events through many centuries; they were designed, not for themselves but for the world, to maintain peace and to make justice prevail among men. For the most part this ideal is felt as a directing spirit. Occasionally it is stated in stirring words as in Book VI, 847–53:

> Let others melt and mould the breathing bronze
> To forms more fair — aye! out of marble bring
> Features that live; let them plead causes well;
> Or trace with pointed wand the cycled heaven,

> And hail the constellations as they rise;
> But thou, O Roman, learn with sovereign sway
> To rule the nations. Thy great art shall be
> To keep the world in lasting peace, to spare
> The humbled foe, and crush to earth the proud.

Professor Woodberry in his noble tribute to Virgil, with one of those sweeping generalizations which eminent students of the poet are so wont to make, speaks of this encomium of Rome as 'the most majestic lines ever written by the hand of man.' Tennyson must have had them in mind when he wrote,

> Though thine ocean-roll of rhythm
> Sound forever of Imperial Rome.

Rome at this moment of her conscious pride needed an interpreter of her better self, one who could reveal her ideal possibilities and summon up her highest mood. Whosoever possesses the capacity to utter the essential spirit of an epoch in a form adequate to the truth renders a service of universal significance. This Homer had done for the heroic age of Greece; this Dante, the voice of ten silent centuries, was to do for the Middle Ages; this Virgil did for the Roman Empire. Alone of all the one hundred and twenty million people comprising the Empire of the day he clearly perceived and established in the thoughts of men the true grandeur that was Rome. He was the embodiment of that national mind at its highest elevation. To him Rome was more than a city of stones and mortar; it was an ideal which should rule in the hearts of all true Romans. The Holy Roman Empire, which was to dominate the courts of Europe for well-nigh two thousand years, was to him, first of all men, actually Holy and Roman and Empire. What was eternal in the grandeur, what was sacred in the Empire, the luminous mind of Virgil sensed and celebrated.

The Story

When his epic was forming itself, Virgil had vividly in his mind the *Iliad* and the *Odyssey*. They were the models which determined the structure of his poem and from which he borrowed incidents, similes, and characters with the utmost freedom. He seems to have contemplated a poem of about ten thousand lines, divided into twelve books.

The general plot of the story is as follows. When Troy fell, Aeneas, a Trojan prince, son of Anchises and Venus, escaped with enough comrades to fill twenty vessels. After beating about the Aegean and Mediterranean seas for six years he was clearly assured by the oracles that Italy was the destined goal. Being in Sicily, he expected to reach Italy in a day or two. Here the *Aeneid* begins. Juno, hating the Trojans, scattered the fleet by a mighty tempest. Aeneas and seven vessels found refuge at Carthage, whose queen, Dido, became enamoured of the leader. The story of her love and sufferings when Aeneas, in obedience to the will of Jupiter, forsakes her to pursue a flying Italy, is among the most celebrated in literature. Then comes a stormy voyage back to Sicily and a quieting interlude of the funeral games before the tomb of Anchises. In the sixth book Aeneas, like Odysseus, goes into the underworld to learn the secrets of the future. Here he beholds the long line of Roman conquerors from Romulus to Caesar, and learns of Rome's divine commission to maintain peace and justice on the earth.

From these experiences Aeneas returns a consecrated man. He knows himself to be an instrument of destiny to carry out the purposes of the Most High. The first six books are strikingly similar to the *Odyssey*. Now the scene changes, and from the seventh book to the end the influence of the *Iliad* is everywhere in evidence. The Trojans land at the mouth of the Tiber, where the King of the Latins receives them kindly, and, that the two people may be united in a common destiny, promises to give his daughter Lavinia to Aeneas to wife. But the wrath of Juno prevents so easy a settlement. The Latins make a desperate effort to drive out the invaders and many glorious deeds of valor are performed. The hero of the Latins falls before Aeneas, and Juno, heart-sick, quits the strife, praying Jove that the descendants of the now united antagonists shall not speak the language or bear the name of Troy, but form the Latin people:

> Let the strong, master blood of Rome receive
> The manhood and the might of Italy,
> Troy perished; let its name and glory die!

And Jove consents:

> Tantae molis erat Romanam condere gentem.   (Bk. I, 33.)
> (So great a labor was it to found the Roman state.)

Perhaps I may best convey what one feels to be the secret of the poetic charm of the *Aeneid* by recalling to the reader the characteristics which Tennyson, out of long study and great love, emphasized. In a sonnet he speaks of the poet's ceaseless labor to perfect his verse;

> Old Virgil who would write ten lines, they say,
> At dawn, and lavish all the golden day
> To make them wealthier in his reader's eyes.

As a result of this discriminating toil his single words had magic in them,

> All the charm of all the Muses flowering in a lonely word.

And 'from many a golden phrase' 'the chosen coin of fancy' flashed out. Supplementing this discriminating selection of words and refinement of phrases, there is the melody of the lines, 'the ocean-roll of rhythm,' making Virgil's Latin hexameters

> ... the stateliest measure
> ever moulded by the lips of man.[1]

The artistic power of the *Aeneid* lies in the magic word, the significant half lines, the stately rhythm, the well-joined structure of the whole, and, shining through all, is the glory of the poet's gracious spirit.

The Spiritual Significance of THE AENEID

The religious value of a great poem lies less in its memorable sentences than in the spirit of the poet. What he is, to borrow a thought from Emerson, speaks more loudly than his verses. The most important influence is that

[1] To Virgil.

which shines through the words and gives to the lines their cadence.

What we find in Virgil, says Warde Fowler, 'more convincingly felt and more resonantly expressed' than in other Latin poets, 'is a kindly and hopeful outlook on the world, with a deep and real sympathy for all sorrow and pain.' [1] Professor Mackail, in his delightful monograph, *Virgil and his Meaning to the World Today*, is equally emphatic: 'In no other poetry are the chords of human sympathy so delicately touched, its tones so subtly interfused. In none is there so deep a sense of the beauty and sorrow of life, of keen remembrance and shadowy hope, and, enfolding all, of infinite pity.' [2] With these judgments all lovers of Virgil will agree. The poet, indeed, because he was following the epic tradition, wrote many pages of battle scenes, but his heart and his genius were not in them. Aeneas slays Lausus with a sad heart, thinking of the boy's mother and how lovingly she wrought his tunic with softest gold (X, 821–30). Again, the warrior turned from lamenting the loss of Pallas, saying

> Ourselves from hence
> Are summoned by the same dread doom of war
> To other tears. (XI, 96.)

Many poets have written on the heroism of battle, its glamour, its stern joy; Virgil, like Euripides, felt the sadness and the pity of it. The expression 'to other tears' inevitably leads our thoughts to that more universal sentence, '*Sunt lacrimae rerum et mentem mortalia tangunt*'

---

[1] *The Religious Experience of the Roman People*, p. 406. [2] Page 110.

(I, 462). The two words *lacrimae rerum*, 'the tears of things,' have been seized upon by succeeding generations as a perfect expression of that element of pain and frustration, that groan of a travailing creation, which is keenly felt by every pitying and lofty soul. Human life seemingly so substantial, yet brief as the fabric of a dream, so lofty in aspiration, so futile in achievement — the great poets have realized the pathos of it all, and have sought to express the 'burthen of the mystery'; but these two words, embedded in Virgil's arresting line, have become the classical utterance of the sad disparity between our ideals and the strange earth we live in. Only from a nature tender and pitying could the enchanted words have come. They voice an aspect of life; they reveal the heart of Virgil. Into the hard, cruel Roman world came, like the first breath of spring after a bitter winter, this gentle influence, persuading a stern race to sympathy, disclosing the beauty and the sadness of life, calling forth all finer sentiments. This is natural religion in its most engaging form, the spirit of Christianity before Christ.

The Character of Aeneas

More concretely, if not more effectually, we learn an author's attitude toward life and its meaning in the character of his hero, especially if the writer is free to create his chief figure and to determine the experiences through which he passes.

This liberty Virgil had in the *Aeneid*. There were vague traditions that Rome was founded by fugitives from Ilium, but the stories lacked authority and had no fixed form in the popular thought. The poet was free to represent a founder having such a character and doing such deeds as would incarnate the ideals which he thought to be most important for the Roman people to imitate. Pious Aeneas is the result. How many schoolboys, in the centuries since Rome fell, have caught a dim vision of him through the unfamiliar Latin! Dim, but decisive. The vast majority have found little to admire. In him there is no dash or color, he utters no words that thrill like a trumpet call. His valor does not shine. A plodding, patient man, ever mindful of his duty, he has been no hero to students.

But the author was not creating a character to fascinate the reader; he was moulding the type of man who had founded Rome and made her great. Romantic leaders who capture the popular imagination are usually better fitted to head a desperate sortie than to found a state. The Hebrews conceived a man of the same qualities as the father of their race. Abraham and Aeneas were conspicuous for the same virtues. Men of duty, obedient to a voice within, they achieved through patient fidelity.

The dominant characteristic of the leader is set forth in the adjective so often applied to him, 'pious.' As Virgil uses the word it means one scrupulously obedient to heaven, faithful in the discharge of his duties to the family and the common good. The pious man is the conscientious man, devout and loyal. By such men Rome was founded and her eminence attained. Such virtues must again be common in Rome, if she would retain her power and establish an ordered society among the nations. This Augustus knew, and this truth Virgil would enforce. Close students have discerned a distinct growth in the character of Aeneas. Devout and loyal from the first, his sense of a divine mission grows clearer and more commanding, and with the deepening consciousness comes added strength and wisdom. The journey among the dead, described in the sixth book, was a crisis in his career. It quickened his sense of a supernatural world and the sure purpose of God. The future life and the responsibility of the individual for his destiny became more real. In him is described the old process — wisdom through suffering. This lesson Sophocles had taught, and Virgil teaches it just as forcibly.

Then there is the ancient truth as conspicuous here as in the *Odyssey*: Odysseus, Aeneas, all men, conquer by meeting triumphantly the successive difficulties which roll in like waves of the sea. The aged Nautes proved his wisdom when he said;

> O goddess-born, we follow here or there,
> As Fate compel or stays. But come what may,
> He triumphs over Fortune, who can bear
> Whate'er she brings. (V, 710.)

The conquering power of toil surrounds the epic like an atmosphere. Aeneas, as he goes to engage in deadly combat with Turnus, whispers the deep secret to his son:

> Disce, puer, virtutem ex me, verumque laborem
> Fortunam ex aliis. (XII, 435.)
>
> (Valor and enduring toil, learn from me, my son;
> the ways of prosperity from others.)

Rome had mastered the world, not by brilliant talents, but by unwearying labor. Rome's greatness did not rest on men like Antony, who sacrificed an empire to his passion for a woman, but on men like Aeneas, who subordinated their desires to the call of duty.

The Divine Purpose

The most distinctive and explicit religious teaching of the epic is its consistent assertion of the providential ordering of events to establish the Roman Empire and ensure a peaceful world. Like the great poet Isaiah, Virgil affirmed that the will of the Supreme Ruler of the world was working through a chosen nation toward a better world order. The thought that Rome should be imperial and rule the nations in justice sounds through all the story. It appears in the second line of the epic in the declaration that Aeneas is an exile of Fate; in the first book Jove declares his fixed decree that the Romans shall be masters of the whole round world, and, clad in peaceful togas, shall judge mankind.

> Then will the world grow mild, the battle sound
> Will be forgot....

Aeneas had an ever deepening conviction that he was a servant of the Most High:

> Whatever be thy name
> Behold we come, O Venerated Power,
> Again with joy we follow! Let thy grace
> Assist us as we go! And may thy power
> Bring none but stars benign across our sky. (IV, 576–79.)

That the destinies of earth are known in heaven is further affirmed by the fact that on the shield which Venus gave Aeneas were emblazoned scenes of the future history of the Roman people. (Book VIII.) Thus we have in the *Aeneid* an aspect of the stern doctrine of foreordination, sung by a Roman poet, as interpreted by Roman history and Roman aspirations.

That the Eternal Spirit has a purpose which he is working out in history through individuals and nations is a fundamental faith in religion. If the High God does not care and help, then comfort and light go out of religion and men are thrown back upon a stark humanism. Virgil wrote under the conviction that Rome would fall short of her divine destiny to maintain peace and justice among men, unless her massive power were linked with ancient piety.

Conclusion

The poet's service to religion was to quicken a sense of a Divine Providence working through the nation for a better world. He also impresses the fundamental truth that man's highest duty is to co-operate with the Divine Will, winning success by overcoming difficulties through virtue and honest labor (*virtutem verumque laborem*). This was his conscious teaching, but it is the unconscious which is the most distinctive and permanently effectual. 'Whoever,' says Lowell, 'can express himself with the full force of unconscious sincerity will be found to have uttered something ideal and universal.' Virgil's most valuable contribution to the life of the spirit in the world was himself. He died before he had perfected the art of his masterpiece, but not before he had uttered himself. Even though the verses were unfinished the splendor shines through, and it is both ideal and universal — a spirit of gentleness and pity, of hope in the presence of life's insoluble problems, of sympathy with all suffering and frustrated people. Such sensitive and noble feeling was not characteristic of the Rome of that period, nor of any other capital. It was a light shining in darkness, a breath from a diviner sphere. It was admired by the Romans of that day, it tempered the rigid austerity of the Latin Fathers of the Church, and has been a constant influence upon the finer spirits of the generations succeeding.

His all-embracing compassion distinguishes Virgil from the pre-Christian poets of the Greco-Roman tradition and has made him one of the heralds of the Christian hope.

The Meaning of Life in the Ancient Poets

WE HAVE been studying the four mightiest poets of the classical world; two representing the Greek and two the Roman civilization. They were gifted above their fellows with power to perceive the beauty of the good earth and the meaning of experience; they were also gifted with superior power to communicate what they thought and felt. 'These abilities,' wrote Milton, 'wheresoever they be found are the inspired gift of God, rarely bestowed, but yet to some (though most abuse) in every Nation.' In them truth lived in attractive imagery, the charm of the musical line, the heroic character.

The first moral truth that emerged and took firm possession of observing minds in ancient days was that there are certain types of conduct, which they called sin or evil, which bring inevitable retribution. The contamination of sin goes down through the family, and its blight falls on one's associates. Sin originates in excess of pride or excess of passion. By great-hearted men it may be forgiven, but not lightly; it must be repented of and expiated. In these early days also there appears prominently the conviction that there is a quality in goodness in heroic souls which in the presence of evil challenges it, triumphs over it, and grows strong and lustrous thereby. This is assumed in Homer and affirmed in Aeschylus.

A youthful zest for life forms the atmosphere of the *Iliad*, and the virtues most admired are courage and wisdom, generosity and kindness. But through both the *Iliad* and the *Odyssey* runs a deep note of sadness: man's days are few and his lot is evil, death is certain, and in Hades he will become a feeble wraith.

Aeschylus, living in a maturer world, finds life more meaningful. He is preoccupied with the majesty and precision of the Moral Order and its just retributions. High Heaven is not unmindful of the righteous, and through suffering comes wisdom.

The Romans were singularly lacking in a sense of the spiritual problems which have so engrossed Greek, Hebrew, and English poets. Lucretius escaped all the difficulties by denying them. Atoms in the grip of universal law are not much concerned with guilt and repentance. Instead of scanning the heights and depths of the soul, he looks out in amazement at the wonders of an orderly universe. His abundant joy is born, not of the thrill of battle, but of a vision of the Infinite Unity flowing eternally. The valor he advocates is not bravery in the face of mortal foe, but a joyful acceptance of the Nature of Things. Yet according to tradition he died by his own hand. Cosmic enthusiasm functions poorly in extreme moments. To convey a sense of universal law, to grapple ably with the tragic folly of superstition, to free men from the fear of death, was a great and permanent contribution to the spiritual treasures of mankind.

The gentle soul of Virgil felt and revealed the beauty of nature, and more energetically than others he proclaimed the dignity of labor and the blessedness of liberty and peace. More than any poet of the West he realized the providential purpose weaving the scattered events of history together. Nevertheless the 'tears of things' were seldom absent from his thoughts. All of these singers seem to be mouthpieces of the dominant spirit of an important epoch. Momentous periods of history culminate in them, and in them find memorable expression. While they mirror civilization it is noteworthy that no one of them takes a rose-colored view of life. They are sensitive to the beauty of the world, they recognize the bravery, the kindness, the nobility of men; yet back of it all, and deeper than all, they feel the sadness of the lot of mortals. Life is short and vain; death is certain and the Elysian Fields are not radiant enough to light up the Dark.

Homer and Lucretius interpreted God, the Ultimate Reality, through Nature and her ways; Aeschylus and Virgil found a clearer revelation in man and human experience. Yet all that they beheld of the divine justice, mercy, and purpose only mitigated the sadness. Greek and Roman alike felt that although the generations of men were playing a drama, not wanting in interest, yet it was a tragedy, and the curtain from which the actors emerged and through which they made their exit was Black.

Dante has put in an unfading picture the impression the ancient world makes upon the reader. Obediently following Virgil, the poet enters Inferno. In the first circle they find a fair land of pleasant air, noble architecture, and lofty conversation. Here dwelt Homer and the famous poets of Rome, 'who spoke seldom and with soft voices.' There was no plaint but that of 'sighs which made the eternal air to tremble,' for they were living 'without hope.' With a few strokes the genius of the Italian has painted the soul of those ancient times. The lords of loftiest song had culture but not a triumphant faith; lacking faith they had no hope. Dante is depicting the spiritual condition of the virtuous and cultured men of antiquity. Matthew Arnold expresses a similar judgment of the ordinary citizen:

> On that hard Pagan world disgust
> And secret loathing fell.
> Deep weariness and sated lust
> Made human life a hell.

One notes also that progress has been made in the spiritual interpretation of man and his world. The supreme God of Virgil is more worthy of his throne than the Zeus of Homer. After Lucretius a Roman would find it more difficult to believe strongly in the capricious deities of his ancestors.

The soul of man, so ghostly in the *Odyssey*, has attained more selfhood when Virgil visits the underworld. But how many needs of man's highest nature are left unsatisfied; how many questions unanswered! The universe seems poorly adjusted to man's many spiritual necessities unless other poets are born with an ampler message.

DANTE: *The Supreme Poet of Christianity*

PROBABLY Virgil's most appreciative reader, the one whom he most profoundly influenced, was a poet greater than himself — Dante Alighieri. Dante imitated him as a poet, admired him as a man, and followed him as a guide through the mazes of moral truth. His admiration breaks forth in spontaneous tributes. Virgil is to him the 'courteous Mantuan,' 'the gentle sage who knew everything,' 'the sea of all wisdom.' At their first meeting in the dark and savage woods Dante exclaims: 'Art thou then that Virgil and that fount which poureth forth so large a stream of speech?... O honor and light of other poets! May the long study avail me and the great love, which have made me search thy volume! Thou art my master and my author; thou alone art he from whom I took the fair style that hath done me honor.' When selecting a guide to lead him through Hell and Purgatory to disciplined liberty he chose Virgil. It may be objected that Virgil in the *Comedy* is a symbol of human reason, yet Dante undoubtedly thought that the Roman poet's graces of character and mellow wisdom made him a most fitting symbol of the human mind at its best.

Dante was no superficial reader. He knew the *Aeneid* practically by heart, and he found in the author deep spiritual meanings. Not only did he find the Messiah predicted in the Fourth Eclogue, he leaned heavily upon Virgil as the inspired interpreter of the divine authority of the Roman Empire, and quoted him with the same confidence he placed in a text of Scripture. He also in the *Comedy* imitated him closely and frequently. Moreover, he discerned in Aeneas those qualities which most adorn manhood — temperance, courage, courtesy, love, and loyalty. This is all set forth in the Fourth Treatise of the unfinished *Convivio*, the twenty-fifth chapter, and in *De Monarchia*, the second book.

But how many storm-swept centuries separate these two kindred spirits! It was in September, 19 B.C., at Brindisi, that the picture of the unrevised *Aeneid* faded from Virgil's brain, and in September, 1321, at Ravenna, Dante 'passed to nobler wars.' Both were Italians, both died on the shores of the Adriatic from exhaustion by their long and exacting labors upon a masterpiece. Between their deaths stretches a span of thirteen hundred and forty years. Living under the same skies, how different their Italy and their world! After Virgil had come the birth of Christ and the beginning of a new era. So well had the Emperor Augustus done his work of stabilizing the Empire that Gibbon could 'fix the period in the history of the world during which the condition of the world was most happy and prosperous' as the years lying between A.D. 96 and 180. With the fifth century came the terrible invasions from the North, the fall of Rome, the confusion of the

DANTE: *The Supreme Poet of Christianity*

Dark Ages, culminating in the power and thought of the thirteenth, one of the most significant of centuries. In this century Dante was born (1265), and his appearance banished the fear that Nature had exhausted her fertility in producing the great poets of Greece and Rome. 'It was as if, at some of the ancient games, a stranger had appeared upon the plain, and thrown his quoit among the marks of former casts which tradition had ascribed to the demi-gods.'[1]

Let us for a moment notice Dante's similarity to his predecessors and his difference from them. Like Homer and Virgil, he is the interpreter of an epoch; more truly so than either of them, for no poem in the world contains so much. In his *Comedy* is the learning, the wisdom, the fears, the superstitions, the romance, the spiritual passions of many centuries. With him a new note becomes strongly evident. His great predecessors had achieved their effects through the majesty and melody of their verses; Dante adds the musical and awakening effects of rhyme. The classic epics were of war and adventure; Dante wrote an epic of spiritual struggle and victory. Since his day no war epic of highest merit has been produced. The greatest of modern poets have placed their battles in the realm of the spirit.

He lacks Homer's zest for life, but he has a far nobler conception of its worth. His sense of the Moral Order is more profound than that of Aeschylus. Like him he might have written tragedy, and that out of his own experience, but he wrote a comedy because he believed in man's power

[1] Hallam, *State of Europe During the Middle Ages.*

131

of victory over evil. Like Lucretius, he was dominated by an instinct for the universal and the infinite; yet, unlike the Roman, he did not seek the mystery of life in its origin; rather he found its explanation in its purpose and its end. Dante took Virgil's theme of the divine mission of the Roman Empire and carried it to a conclusion of which that poet never dreamed. He was not inferior to the Roman in his feeling for 'the tears of things,' yet in sublimity of imagination, depth, and range of thought he easily surpassed the poet whom he called his master.

In a true sense he is the first modern man. In his *De Vulgari Eloquentia* he wrote the first modern critical study of language; he had the courage to commit his greatest work to the vulgar tongue; in *De Monarchia* he wrote a most important book advocating the separation of the Church and State with a wisdom which is only recently having its effect; his tremendous individualism has been a revolutionary force of constant influence. Dante thought himself to have been born in an evil time; in reality he came at the culminating point of the old order and the beginning of the new, and of both he was a great part.

What We Know of Dante

Our best knowledge of the poet we gain from his published works, which are marvelously self-revealing. Next in importance are his early biographers. One, Giovanni Villani, was a contemporary, who lived in Florence and kept a chronicle of affairs in his native city. The closing words of his account of the poet bring him very near:

DANTE: *The Supreme Poet of Christianity*

'This Dante, from his knowledge was somewhat presumptuous, harsh, and disdainful, like an ungracious philosopher; he scarcely deigned to converse with laymen; but for his other virtues, science, and worth as a citizen, it seems most reasonable to give him perpetual remembrance in this our chronicle: nevertheless, his noble works, left us in writing, bear true testimony to him, and honorable fame to our city.'

Another source is the famous Boccaccio, who, only eight years old when Dante died, became a devoted admirer of his genius. Besides lecturing on the *Comedy*, he wrote from source-material a life of Dante which was excellent. He had access to many friends of the poet, and knew Dante's nephew and Dante's daughter, Beatrice, to whom he was the bearer of ten florins of gold, a gift from the city of Florence. Although somewhat garrulous, he has written an interesting *Vita di Dante*, which is on the whole dependable.

From these original sources, and from the researches of scholars in the *Comedy* and in the archives of Italy, the following outline is derived.

Dante Alighieri was born in Florence in the year 1265, and died in Ravenna in 1321. The family was of the lesser nobility, and gave to the dark-eyed boy the best education the city afforded. When he was nine years old, as he tells us in the *Vita Nuova*, he met a girl slightly younger, 'clothed in a most noble crimson.' The lad was deeply smitten, and henceforth Love lorded it over his life. Nine years later, at a chance meeting, the maiden saluted him with such ineffable courtesy that he seemed to touch all the bounds of bliss. This Lady of the Salutation he calls Beatrice, the blessed one. This name he may have given her to hide her identity, or she may have been an ideal, the lady of his mind; but the weight of evidence seems to decide that she was Beatrice Portinari, daughter of a prominent burger of Florence, and later the wife of Simone de' Bardi.

Returning to his room, he wrote a sonnet, celebrating a vision of Love, and sent it to a group of young Florentine poets whom he calls 'liegemen of Love.' The designation is full of meaning. The poetry of courtly love, as sung by the troubadours, had become conventional, and in Tuscany had been supplanted by a finer conception, clothed in verse far more ethereal. Love was not the passion of a man for a maid, it was the aspiration of a gentle heart for an ideal beauty. The Lady was the medium through which divine loveliness reached the lover's heart. She may have been but a chance acquaintance, or even a married woman. This was immaterial. Through her the ray of beauty had kindled the mind of the poet, and in her as a symbol he celebrated a glorious ideal. This was a mood too lofty for most of the young gallants of Florence, and they were continually falling from this spiritual stratosphere to much more earthly levels.

Dante's wings proved strong enough to sustain him in the high altitude. During some seven years, he found his satisfaction in acclaiming the glories of his lady. Then, when he was twenty-five, Beatrice died. To Dante desolation fell upon the city; but instead of writing a threnody of his sorrow he began pondering, in true medieval fashion, the mystical significance of numbers. He was nine years old when he first met Beatrice; at the time of her most sweet salutation he was eighteen; she died on the ninth day of the month, in the ninth month of the year, and in the year of the century when the perfect number ten had been completed for the ninth time. That is, she died an hour after sunset on the eighth of June, 1290. He also declared that at her birth the nine heavens were in perfect relations. In his thought, not only was she accompanied by the mystical blessings of the number nine, she was a Nine! i. e. a miracle, for her beauty was rooted in the Trinity even as the number nine is three multiplied by itself. Thus is this Lady of the Salutation apotheosized into a miracle of God. The light in her eyes was a demonstration of the Divine Truth; the sweetness of her smile was persuasive of Divine Love.

A few years later, Dante gathered the sonnets and *canzoni* which he had written in praise of Beatrice, explained their meaning in quaint prose commentaries, and published them in a slender volume under the title of *Il Vita Nuova* ('The New Life'). It is one of the world's most famous love stories. Six hundred years have scarcely dimmed its charm. The closing words are memorable for beauty and prophecy:

> After this sonnet, a wonderful vision appeared to me, in which I saw things which made me resolve to speak no more of this blessed one until I could more worthily treat of her. And to attain to this, I study to the utmost of my power, as she truly knows. So that, if it shall please Him through whom all things live, that my life be prolonged for

some years, I hope to say of her what was never said of any woman.

And then may it please Him who is the Lord of Grace, that my soul may go to behold the glory of its lady, namely, of that blessed Beatrice, who in glory looks upon the face of Him *qui est per omnia saecula benedictus* [who is blessed forever].

Thereafter he studied diligently, engaged in the gaieties, the wars, the politics of Florence, and was married to Gemma, a member of the powerful house of Donati. In the year 1300 he became one of the six priors, or rulers, of the city. It was a fateful year, and to it he attributed all his misfortunes. His political enemies coming into power soon afterwards, he was banished and sentenced to be burned alive, if ever he returned to 'that fair fold where as a lamb he had been folded.' Henceforth he wandered about Italy, and perhaps beyond her border, finding how hard it is to climb another's stairs, and how salt is the bread of strangers.

Things were going wrong in the political world. More profoundly and passionately even than Virgil, Dante believed that the Roman Empire was of God, created and preserved to establish justice upon earth. To it belonged supreme temporal dominion, and to the Church authority in things spiritual. In his thought the woes of Europe were largely due to the disastrous meddling of the Church in temporal affairs — the sword was jointed to the crozier. He believed that the Holy Roman Empire lived in the person of Henry VII of Luxemburg, and that peace would come to distracted Italy only when the people recognized the temporal supremacy of the Empire, and the Church was satisfied with spiritual dominion. In defense of this ideal Dante wrote his justly famous treatise entitled *De Monarchia*. Although Henry was crowned in the Lateran in Rome, Italy still resisted his claim to sovereignty, and, worn out by constant disappointment, Henry died in the summer of 1313.

For Dante the cup of bitterness was full, and, realizing that he was groping in a savage wood of public sin and political intrigue, he returned for refuge to his studies and to poetry — to Virgil and to Beatrice, and to that unfulfilled pledge to say of her what had never been said of any woman.

The *Comedy* may have been simmering in his mind during these years of political activity. He may have written sections of it. But I believe that in the year 1313, when his political hopes collapsed, the poet set himself with full devotion to utter his deepest convictions in a poem that should not die.

Besides writing *De Monarchia*, he had begun before 1309 a treatise on love and virtue entitled *Il Convivio* ('the Banquet'), which he never finished, and a learned critique of Italian dialects entitled *De Vulgari Eloquentia* ('On the Common Speech'). This also was never completed.

After a prolonged stay in Verona, the poet at length appeared, about 1317, in Ravenna, which was his last refuge. In this city, rich in traditions and architectural memorials, surrounded by friends and, for at least part of the time, by his children, the poet completed his immortal poem. Whether he ever gave it a final revision is uncertain, for soon after the text was finished he went to Venice on a mission from the Lord of Ravenna. Unsuccessful in his purpose, he returned overland through a malarial district. Worn out by the journey, exhausted still more by his arduous labors on the *Paradiso*, the fever he had contracted met but a feeble resistance and, a few days after his return, he died in Ravenna in the night between September 13 and 14, 1321. And there his ashes remain unto this day.

Dante's Sense of Prophetic Mission

There were three urges impelling Dante to utter himself in a long poem. He was a poet, fully conscious of possessing extraordinary capacities, ambitious of recognition, and eager to achieve the highest excellence; he was a lover who would say of his lady what had never been said of any woman; he was a prophet, burdened like the seers of Israel with an authentic message from the Most High concerning the political evils of the times. We are accustomed to think of Dante as poet and lover, but are apt to forget how tremendous was his conviction of his prophetic mission. He was making no inquisitive journey into the eternal world merely to gather poetic material for a masterpiece. 'Down through a world of endless bitterness,' over the mountain of pain, up through the revolving heavens he journeyed that he might learn the truth and cast its intense light upon the problems of earth. As with the prophets, anger against sin burned like a fire in his bones, and like them he constrained his passion to his art. He polished his thunderbolts. He did not furiously hack and mar his victims, he carved them up, a feast fit for the gods. Even in the highest heaven he does not forget to turn its full light upon the iniquities of earth. And his final prayer as he joins his gaze to the Eternal Fountain is that he may not fail of his appointed task:

> O Supreme Light, that so high upliftest Thyself from mortal conceptions, relend a little to my mind of what Thou didst appear, and make my tongue so powerful that it may be able to leave one single spark of Thy glory for the future people, for, by returning somewhat to my memory and by sounding a little in these verses, more of Thy victory shall be conceived.

The Meaning of THE COMEDY

Fortunately for this inquiry, we have Dante's own un-equivocal statement. In his letter to Can Grande, his powerful friend in Verona, he declares that it is called a comedy because it is written in the humble tongue of the people and has a happy ending. Moreover the work has many meanings, 'for there is one meaning that is derived from the letter and another that is derived from the things indicated by the letter. The first is called *literal*, but the second *allegorical* or *mystical*.' The literal interpretation gives us a description of the state of souls after death, but 'the subject of the whole work, allegorically considered, is man, liable to the reward and punishment of Justice, according as through the freedom of the will he is deserving or undeserving.'

The literal meaning belongs to the age in which the scenes were described, and does not now concern us. It is the spirit contained in the form which has permanent interest. Interpreted as a well thought out allegory, we have in the *Comedy* a great mind's picture of the meaning of life, painted against the background of the eternal world, so that all beginnings may be seen in their final fruition.

The key to this deeper significance is found in the opening canto of the *Inferno*. 'Midway upon the road of our life' Dante found himself in a dark wood, for the right way had been missed. Arriving at the foot of a hill whose summit was crowned with light, he began the ascent. He would escape from this savage wood of personal sin and political intrigue to the liberty and light of the Delectable Mountain. But a leopard, symbol of the licentious impulses of the flesh, hindered him. Then a lion, type of violent and wilful sins, came against him. More formidable still, a she-wolf, representing the deadly sins of the spirit, 'pushed me back to where the sun is silent.' While in black despair at the foot of the mountain, before his eyes appeared one 'who through long silence seemed hoarse.' It is Virgil, personification of perfected human reason; Virgil, whose long-neglected message of the divine authority of the Roman Empire made his word seem but a whisper. The Roman poet offers to be Dante's guide through the pit of the lost souls, and up over the mountain of Purgatory. From there, he promises, Beatrice will reveal the glories of the spiritual life in an ascent from heaven to heaven until the poet shall look into the Fountain of Living Light Eternal.

This is the outline of the poem's movement. The *Inferno*

is not a horrible picture of torments, devised by the fiendish
ingenuity of a medieval schoolman. It is the portrayal of
the nature and consequences of sin by one whom Lowell
has called 'the highest spiritual nature that has expressed
itself in rhythmical form.' Dante, urged by the prophet's
fire in his bones, would arouse a misguided world to the
character of sin and its sure results. Let the theologians
wrangle over their definitions, he will paint sin in colors
so vivid and powerful that its real nature will stand revealed in its grisly horror. To do this he must go among
the 'truly dead' where sin is known in its ultimate condition.

The INFERNO

The *Inferno* is a descent into the world's sin — sin as it
was in Italy in the thirteenth century, sin as it is today
among modern men. Its essential nature is revealed in
three ways: by depicting the sinner given over to his be-
setting fault, by placing him in an environment which
symbolizes his guilt, and by personifying the sin in the
demons who preside over the nine concentric circles of the
underworld — an underworld which Dante conceives as
a vast conical-shaped cavity, located directly under Mount
Calvary and the Cross, thus declaring in a most powerful
manner the defeat of Satan.

Dante probably believed with his time that hell is a
place, but his perpetual message is that hell is a condition
of soul; man is punished, not *for* his sins but *by* them; the
evil soul creates its own environment; sin is monstrous,

stupid, and finally ridiculous. There were three beasts on the mountain; there are three zones in hell — of darkness, fire, and arctic cold. For sin, ignorant and blind, drains down into fiery torment and finally into spiritual death.

The underlying philosophy of the *Inferno* and of the two subsequent divisions is clearly expressed in the opening of the third canto

> ... Through me is the way into the woeful city; through me is the way into the eternal woe; through me is the way among the lost people. Justice moved my lofty maker: the divine Power, the supreme Wisdom, and the primal Love made me. Before me were no things created, unless eternal, and I eternal last. Leave every hope, ye who enter.
>
> These words of color obscure I saw written at the top of the gate; whereat I: 'Master, their meaning is dire to me.'
>
> And he to me, like one who knew: 'Here it behoves to leave every fear; it behoves that every cowardice should here be dead. We have come to the place where I have told thee that thou shalt see the woeful people, who have lost the good of the understanding.'

Following the Scriptures and the saints, Dante maintains that the good of the understanding is the contemplation of God. The supreme blessedness is to know God. Sin blinds the intellect so that it fails to discern His justice and love working through one's experience and in the courses of the world. This leaves one in an Inferno of helpless woe. To lay hold of the truth that Wisdom, Justice, and Love are working through one's sufferings gives them a purifying value; the ever-deepening vision of the Divine leads one up steadily to the Ultimate Beatitude. This is the structural philosophy of the whole

Comedy. To know God is life eternal. When one is insensible to his presence one is in a hopeless state which leads downwards to woe; when one perceives a divine Purpose operating in his experience life becomes a purgatorial process; the enlarging consciousness of the Divine is the spirit's paradise.

As Virgil leads Dante downwards through the narrowing circles of Hell, they have many thrilling adventures. They listen to the piteous story of Francesca, they secretly admire Farinata, holding 'Hell in great scorn,' they meet Brunetto Latini, Dante's beloved teacher, to whom he paid this marvelous tribute: 'In the world, hour by hour, you taught me how man makes himself eternal.' And at the center of the earth they find Satan, not the Lord of Hell, but its prisoner, frozen forever in the lake of tears and blood which flow down from the earth to imprison the great Perpetrator. Dante's description of Satan is his final judgment on the essential nature of sin; in its ultimate condition it is without attraction, it is ugly, foul, stupidly brutal, ludicrous.

The PURGATORIO

It is Easter morning of the year 1300 when the two poets come to the foot of a glorious mountain, situated in an imagined hemisphere of water opposite to Jerusalem, where souls are purified and restored to primal innocence. In conceiving Purgatory as a mountain, not a dungeon of torment, Dante showed genuine originality, for souls are cleansed and vivified by the ministries of art, horizons, music. All true life is a climb upward and liberty lies at the top; it is an achievement, not a donation; it is won by sternest discipline.

Before they begin the ascent Dante's face is washed by the dews of repentance and he is girded with the reeds of humility. He passes through anti-Purgatory, where spirits expiate the years wasted in unrepentance, and comes to a gate before which lie three steps, one clear as a mirror, one rough, one red as blood, representing the three steps necessary to justification: confession, contrition, satisfaction. The angel on guard cuts seven P's on Dante's forehead, indicative of the seven mortal sins which must be purged on the seven successive ledges rising before him. Then at the summit, free and upright, he becomes king and bishop of his own soul. He has attained the original innocence of Adam and the glorious liberty of the children of God. Virgil (Reason), having disclosed the nature of sin and the way of purification, can lead no further and must return to the underworld, to the company of Homer and the virtuous spirits of antiquity. Dante's rigid creed makes the parting necessary, but he shows his undying honor to the Roman poet by representing the angels accompanying Beatrice as singing some of Virgil's own lines. What greater satisfaction could a poet have than to know that his songs were repeated in heaven? The philosophy underlying the construction of this section of the poem is of perpetual validity, and therefore modern. The spirit of man naturally loves the good and runs toward it, but it mistakes trivial and momentary good for something of permanent worth.

It loves the wrong objects. What is supremely needed is to set love in order — love which is either excessive, defective, or perverted. This is done by fixing one's attention on the true nature of the virtue to be acquired and practicing it. Thought becomes act; act grows into a habit; habit solidifies into character.

The significance of Beatrice, who appears to the poet at the summit, cannot be fully stated in a word. But as she comes in a chariot which I take to represent the visible Church, she is to my mind the personification of what the Church brings to humanity. She is Divine Revelation with all the glory and power belonging thereto. This is in accord with the theological thinking of that day. Human reason being incapable of penetrating the divine mysteries, it is supplemented by divine revelation.

The PARADISO

The *Paradiso*, which Dante called 'the sublime canticle,' is the supreme triumph of his artistic genius; indeed, it is the loftiest and most sustained flight of the spiritual imagination in literature. 'It is no coasting voyage,' he exclaims, 'this which the intrepid prow goes cleaving, nor for a pilot who would spare himself,' and he pleads that he well may be pardoned, if under the ponderous burden his mortal shoulder trembles.

The theme in its literal interpretation is a journey up through the nine heavens, recognized by the astronomy of the day, to the Empyrean, the timeless, spaceless region, where God and the redeemed dwell in full felicity.

Allegorically it presents the soul of the believer under the guidance of Divine Revelation moving through sphere after sphere of knowledge and blessedness to attain the final beatitude of perfect union with the Love which pervades the universe. The spirits whom the poet meets in the different heavens are the redeemed, descending to welcome him as he ascends the stairway of worlds which lead from earth to highest heaven. The force which urges the spirit upwards is the perpetual thirst for God. The poet moves, not by conscious motion, but by beholding the ever-enhancing beauty of the face of Beatrice. What better way of describing the soul's growth in spiritual things than by the increasing appreciation of 'the glory of truth enkindled along the stairway of the Eternal Palace.' It is such a heaven as Sir Isaac Newton might have imagined, ever-deepening knowledge quickening intense love, and heightening love stimulating ever more eager service. It is not a heaven with streets of gold and gates of pearl, but a condition of the soul growing in the knowledge of God and in the joys of union with him.

The Beatific Vision

The crowning glory of the *Paradiso* is the Beatific Vision as related in the final cantos of this strange and marvelous book. 'No uninspired hand' says Cardinal Manning, 'has ever written thoughts so high in words so resplendent as the last canto of the *Divina Commedia.*' One cannot enter into the High Mood there expressed, or feel its suggestive and unearthly splendor by a casual reading. He must have followed Dante, step by step through the arduous journey, mounting from light to light, from virtue to virtue, until his whole being is attempered to the celestial truth and rapture. Even Dante's superhuman power proves inadequate to describe the ineffable experience. So he resorts to symbols to hint at what his tongue cannot utter. How few and simple they are! A point, a circle, light intensified to its highest glory.

Having ascended through the nine heavens, he enters the Empyrean, a place of 'light intellectual full of love, love of true good full of joy, joy that transcends every sweetness,' where God and the saints have their dwelling-place. What symbol can he find in earth or heaven to give the truest idea of the Everlasting? Dante is too wise to represent the Limitless anthropomorphically as a benevolent father or a king on his throne, as do the artists and many poets. Failing to find an appropriate suggestion for the infinitely large, he goes to the opposite extreme and chooses the infinitely small — a point of light. Now, a point is omnipresent, indivisible, incorporeal, incomprehensible; its center is everywhere and its circumference nowhere. Move the point and we have a line, swing the line and we have a circle, revolve the circle and we have a sphere. What more meaningful symbol is there of Him who is the source and center of all, the omnipresent fountain of life, than a point 'so keen that the sight on which it shines must needs close because of its intense keenness?'

The redeemed are assembled in the form of a great white rose, and are looking with joyful faces at the Point which, high above them (for the poet must use spacial terms to describe the spaceless), sheds its supernal brightness upon them, and forms in the center of the Rose what seems to Dante a lake of golden light.

Turning to question Beatrice, he beholds, instead of her beautiful face, a venerable old man, 'robed like the saints in glory.' It is Saint Bernard, type of Spiritual Intuition; for the pilgrim no longer needs the aid of Revelation, he will see with direct penetration into the unveiled truth. Bernard offers a prayer of singular lyrical beauty to the Virgin that she will grant to her faithful one the vision which brings all blessedness. Dante, looking upwards, finds that his

> sight, becoming pure, was entering more and more through the radiance of the lofty Light, which in Itself is true.... I saw that in its depth is enclosed, bound up with love in one volume, that which is dispersed in leaves through the universe; substance and accidents and their modes, fused together, as it were, in such wise, that that of which I speak is one simple Light.... Thus my mind, wholly rapt, was gazing fixed, motionless, intent, and ever with gazing grew enkindled. In that Light one becomes such that it is impossible he should ever consent to turn himself from it for other sight; because the Good which is the object of the will is all collected in it, and outside of it that is defective which is perfect there.... Within the profound and clear subsistence of the lofty Light appeared to me three circles of three colors and of one dimension; and the one seemed reflected by the other, as Iris by Iris.... That circle which appeared in Thee generated as a reflected light, being awhile surveyed by my eyes, seemed to me depicted with our effigy within itself, of its own very color; wherefore my sight was wholly set upon it.... I wished to see how the image was conformed to the circle, and how it has its place therein, but my own wings were not for this, had it not been

that my mind was smitten by a flash in which its wish came.

To the high fantasy here power failed, but now my desire and my will were revolved, like a wheel that is moved evenly, by the Love which moves the sun and other stars.

Translating this vision into the speech of today, it means that the truest blessedness the spirit of man can attain is keen awareness that a divine Love penetrates and enfolds all things, and that our humanity is grounded in the Eternal, and the Eternal lives in us. To know this, and to center one's life perfectly upon it — this is the supreme beatitude. Beyond this there is no blessedness, either in this world or the world to come.

The above is but a meager outline of the *Paradiso*. Much of the book is difficult to read because its medieval interests are not vital today. But there are passages which glow with undying fire, and truths of the utmost import in all centuries. There is that immortal sentence which Piccarda uttered in the lowest heaven: '... and his will is our peace.' There is Dante's confident affirmation that man may know spiritual truth:

> Well I perceive that never sated is
> Our intellect unless Truth illumine it,
> Beyond which nothing true expands itself.
> It rests therein, as wild beast in his lair,
> When it attains it; and it can attain it;
> If not, then each desire would frustrate be.

Equally certain is he of man's essential freedom: 'The greatest gift which God in his bounty bestowed in creating, and the most conformed to his own goodness, and that which he prizes most, was freedom of the will.' And again:

'... the free will, which if it endure fatigue in the first battles with the heavens, afterwards, if it be well nurtured, conquers everything.'

The political element in the *Divine Comedy* must not go unmentioned, for the latter is one of the most powerful controversial documents ever written. In his journey through the three realms Dante is constantly discussing political conditions and denouncing the sins of his time. When in Paradise, he is continually turning supernal light down on the dark practices of men here below. What more effective method could a reformer invent to bring home to men the corrupt deeds of the papal authorities than to show the white light of heaven turn red with anger as Saint Peter himself denounces his successors for turning Rome into a sewer of filth? And the very last words uttered by Beatrice — 'sweet guide and dear' — as she turned to gaze upon the Fountain of Eternal Light, was to pronounce, from the highest heaven, a condemnation of Pope Clement V to the third *bòlgia* of the eighth circle of hell, pushing deeper in torment Boniface VIII. Certainly righteous wrath could not be expressed more dramatically or more impressively to a fourteenth-century audience. No writer has equaled Dante in ability to turn politics into art, and to capitalize the authority of the mighty dead. No one has approached him in power to bring the sanctions of the Eternal to bear on the trivial concerns of earth, to make the judgment seat of the Almighty turn the noisy currents of history.

DANTE: *The Supreme Poet of Christianity*

The Permanent Spiritual Values of
THE COMEDY

The author called his work 'The Comedy'; successive generations of readers have added the adjective 'Divine,' for they have discerned in it a permanent element of extraordinary value. To every Dante-lover there is an arresting beauty glowing through the poet's sentences. They are mindful of the vivid and ineffaceable pictures, the lines precise as a statement in Euclid, the sentiments infinitely delicate and full of grace, and the glare of terrible passions. The theology they find may be utterly alien to them, but one cannot live in the atmosphere of the poet's world and think his thoughts without having created in one's mind those exalted moods which make life worth living.

Beyond the poetical enchantment of the verses there are three values, enduring and of conspicuous worth, to which I wish to call the reader's attention. First, the profound and startling impression the book leaves on the mind of the reader that man lives in a Moral Order which is vigilant, instant, inexorable. One feels that the story is not the romance of a brilliant imagination but a transcript of reality, and that he is face to face with the undoubted experience of the race. The *Inferno* is not a nightmare of horror; it is a presentation of experienced truth. There are spiritual conditions which darken the mind, are sterile as sand, tormenting as fire, cold as a lake of frozen tears. The *Purgatorio* is true. Liberty is an achievement; it lies at the top of the mountain and is reached by those who, through severe discipline, 'set love in order.' The *Paradiso* is true. Man does not climb into spiritual felicity; he ascends by faith — faith which is insight, insight plus valor, and his supreme beatitude is to behold the glory of truth and to be centered on it.

The second value is Dante's interpretation of God and human life in terms of love. The popular notion is that the Florentine is conspicuous for his vindictive wrath. Quite the contrary. He is one of the world's most famous lovers, and the *intelletto d'amore* is the central theme of his poetry from the first pages of the *Vita Nuova* to the last page of the *Commedia*. Love first awoke him to poetry; the love of a maiden revealed the love which is enthroned on high. In his philosophy the Primal Love ordained the penalties of evil. The opening sentence of the *Paradiso* declares that the glory of this love 'penetrates the universe and is resplendent in one part more and in another less.' And his vision of the Ultimate Reality reveals that love binds all things into one volume. Love penetrates and unites all forces and experiences; it moves the sun and other stars, and the wills of all who are blessed. Dante is consistently and pre-eminently the poet of love.

The third value is his firm and inspiring assurance of the possibility of living a victorious life. Homer, in spite of the joy he found in living, looked sadly upon human fate. The greatest dramatists of Athens wrote tragedy. Dante had all the material in his own bitter experience, and in the wickedness of the world about him, to write one of the world's gloomiest tragedies. Instead he wrote hu-

manity's most significant comedy. He could do this because he had — what none of his predecessors in the great
Succession possessed — in equal degree and with equal
confidence, a belief in the freedom of the human will and
the richness of the divine Grace. These lift man out of
the order of necessity, make possible victory over adverse
fortunes, and out of tragedy emerge triumphant. If one's
choices are right, wide are the arms of Divine Mercy, and
the resources of help are abundant and ever near. Through
grace the free moral will of man may win the battle. The
same immortal strain that sounds in the eighth chapter of
Romans and the fifteenth of Corinthians sounds throughout the *Comedy*. Excepting the Scriptures, no poet of any
age or country has equaled Dante in interpreting life in its
victorious aspects. None has traced so clearly the way
through a hell of darkness, through the purifying disci-
plines obtained by obeying love rightly placed, to ever-
increasing blessedness by trusting those truths and energies which are apprehended by our highest spiritual
faculties.

I cannot close this chapter better than by quoting the
memorable words with which Lowell closes his essay on
Dante:

> At the Round Table of King Arthur there was always left
> one seat empty for him who should accomplish the adven-
> ture of the Holy Grail. It was called the perilous seat, be-
> cause of the dangers he must encounter who would win it.
> In the company of the epic poets was a place left for who-
> ever should embody the Christian ideal of a triumphant
> life, outwardly all defeat, inwardly victorious, who should
> make us partakers of that cup of sorrow in which all are

communicants with Christ. He who should do this would indeed achieve the perilous seat, for he must combine poesy with doctrine in such cunning wise that the one lose not its beauty and the other its severity, and Dante has done it. As he takes possession of it we seem to hear the cry he himself heard when Virgil rejoined the company of great singers —

All honor to the loftiest of poets!

SHAKESPEARE: *What He Admired and What He Believed*

In passing from Dante to Shakespeare we are conscious of entering an entirely different world. We have the feeling of one who leaves a solemn cathedral, with its mystic shadows and haunting symbolism, and steps out into an open country of spacious and varied landscape, glorious with sunshine and black thunderclouds, and meets eagerly a crowd of most interesting people.

The two poets have marked contrasts. Dante is 'world-high and world-deep; Shakespeare is world-wide.' Dante was a poet-prophet dominated by a lofty ambition to make his whole vision manifest. He made himself lean for many years that by 'long study and great love' he might leave a name that would be familiar to the future people. Shakespeare was more haphazard; the love of fame was certainly not a prevailing motive. 'He wrote,' says Hazlitt, 'for the great vulgar and the small, in his time. If Queen Elizabeth and the maids of honor laughed heartily at his worst jokes, and the catcalls in the gallery were silent at his best passages, he went home satisfied, and slept the next night well.' Dante was austere; Shakespeare gentle. Dante died poor and in debt; Shakespeare acquired abundant possessions. The Italian was supremely interested in religion and the life after death; the Englishman was too thoroughly in love with life to give prolonged thought to metaphysical speculation. Dante was one of the most learned men of his time; Shakespeare made a little learning go far.

It has often been said that Shakespeare's genius was so extraordinary that he effectually conceals himself and his real outlook upon life. It is his characters who speak and not he. This can hardly be true. The speech of a dramatist will betray him. If Apollo should assume mortal form, there would be moments when his speech would transcend his disguise; supernal glory would occasionally shine through. Shakespeare reveals himself in the management of his plots, the characters he chooses and delights in, the spirit in which he touches his theme, the atmosphere he creates, in the splendor of thought and metaphor which are infinitely beyond the capacity of the character who utters them. Shakespeare is not concealed by the creatures of his imagination. A very distinct image of him has been impressed upon the generations of his readers. Indeed, so indubitably does he manifest his principles, his tempers, and his delights that we are able to trace his artistic and spiritual development and recognize some of the influences which molded him.

The known facts of the poet's life are not as abundant as we might wish, but they are sufficient, I think, for us to trace his intellectual and spiritual progress and win some perception of the sources of his growing wisdom.

We know that this son of John Shakespeare, one time High Bailiff of Stratford, was baptized in the village church April 26, 1564. In his nineteenth year he was married to Anne Hathaway, who was six years his senior, and his daughter Susanna was baptized some six months later at Stratford. The church books also record that his twin children, Hamnet and Judith, received the rite of baptism February 2, 1585, according to modern reckoning. It is the common opinion that in his early twenties he went up to London to seek his fortune. He carried with him some learning found in books, but he was far richer in knowledge of the habits, speech, and beliefs of the people. Within him also was a strong love of the beauties of the English countryside and a lively curiosity concerning the ways and motives of men. By nature he was high-spirited and of a genial temper, yet his ardor for the new adventure must have been steadied by some very sober thoughts. Young as he was, he had a wife and three children dependent upon him, and the family fortunes were low. The light-hearted days of youth were over, and earnest effort must be made if he was to win the position among his fellows which he craved. Did the most comprehensive and penetrating imagination that ever looked on London streets visualize his future as an enchanted land, or was it gloomy with forebodings?

We may be confident that he turned immediately to the theater for work. Authorities differ regarding the company which first employed him, but they agree that soon he found a place among the actors, appearing in minor parts and assisting in the preparation of plays.

Necessarily these apprentice years, spent in learning his craft, were years of drudgery, hack work, and discipline. Pope's couplet is as superficial as it is flashing:

> For gain, not glory, wing'd his roving flight
> And grew immortal in his own despight.

This judgment is certainly misleading. Genius, however extraordinary, cannot dispense with the training that comes from hard work, both in gathering material and in gaining mastery of one's tools. To use a retort credited to Daniel Webster, 'There is no such thing as extemporaneous acquisition.' In his earliest plays, *Love's Labour's Lost* and *The Comedy of Errors*, there are indications that he has studied extensively the Italian school of drama. *Henry VI* shows him familiar with Marlow. *Titus Andronicus* witnesses to his study of Seneca and the Roman drama.

These years of experimentation discredit the notion that the getting of riches was his dominant ambition. Rather do they represent him eager to explore and develop his artistic capacities and to perfect his workmanship. To find himself, to understand life in its multifarious aspects, to present it effectively, these held no inferior place in his ambition. If we consider the years of his apprenticeship as ending in 1594 when he was thirty years of age, we have evidence of the severity of his toil and the variety of his experiments. He had tested his genius in two long poems, *Venus and Adonis* and *The Rape of Lucrece*. He had written, collaborated in, or gloriously revised three comedies, *Love's Labour's Lost*, *The Comedy of Errors*, *Two*

Gentlemen of Verona, one faery play, *Midsummer Night's Dream,* and the first draft of *Romeo and Juliet.* He had broadened his knowledge, and disciplined his mind by producing six historical plays. His success was arousing jealousy in the world of the theater. According to Greene this 'conceited Shakescence' was 'able to bumbast out a blank verse with the best.' The mere task of writing out in longhand so many plays is somewhat appalling, yet he was looking for new tests of his powers and was sub-duing his exuberant genius to the niceties of the sonnet form. By the end of 1594 he was producing better plays and writing more beautiful sonnets than any writer of his time. His flight, indeed, was somewhat roving, but it was moving with a well-defined and mastering purpose. That dominant purpose was neither gain nor glory, but to find himself and know his world. One ability he had discovered in himself in which he became pre-eminent, namely, the ability to understand, analyze, and portray character.

The years following, extending from 1594 to 1600, often called his second period, are conspicuous for three im-mortal characters, Shylock, Henry V, and Falstaff. Brutus also stands within this period. The years between 1590 and 1600 are bound together by their dominant mood. They are marked by a zest for life, spontaneous mirth, delight in the sword-play of keen and flashing wit. It is true that the darker side of life is not absent, but life as a whole looks radiant. The author's spirits were buoyant; fancies darted from his fertile brain as sparks fly from an anvil. One must have been very well, very happy, and

very young even to think of celebrating the cold gray
dawn with such words as

> Night's candles are burnt out, and jocund day
> Stands tiptoe on the misty mountain-tops.

What wisdom of the higher sort did Shakespeare gather
during those ten years of discipline and self-discovery?
What does he communicate to us out of them? I think he
learned much through his prolonged meditation in the
preparation and writing of the historical plays. In these
he is not content with putting a pageant on the stage; he
searches for the secrets of character and the elements
of royal success and failure. Professor Dowden finds in
them a marked disclosure of the dramatist's personality.
Although dealing with historical events, he cannot escape
himself, but must perforce organize his facts around his
strongest feelings and most cherished convictions re-
specting human life.[1] He has given us six full-length
portraits of kings of England. These six fall into groups of
three each. One, *King John*, *Richard II*, *Henry VI*, consists of studies of kingly weakness; the other, *Henry IV*,
Henry V, *Richard III*, are sketches of kingly strength.
He finds that the defects of kings have consequences
which are not confined to themselves: they move out in
wide devastation. Wrongdoing brings its inevitable retribution. The harvest follows the sowing. Crime is disastrous, but so is weakness. The saintliness of Henry VI and
the gentle sentimentality of Richard II lead to failure.
Neither Aeschylus nor Sophocles have more clearly as-

---

[1] *Shakespeare, His Mind and Art*, p. 145.

serted the sure penalties following wrong doing or error. Richard III achieves because of the singleness of his purpose and the fertile energy of his will. No scruples deter him, no sympathies hamper him. His eye is single, therefore he is strong. But the audacious strength of intelligent will cannot cope with the moral structure of the universe. The stars in their courses are against him. In the final battles the spiritual forces are all with Richmond.

Shakespeare's sense of right and wrong was naturally exquisite and lofty, and this prolonged study in English history deepened his belief in the moral framework of the world. Evildoing does not long succeed; it disintegrates character, it dulls the mind, it leads to folly. He discerned in history and made evident in his historical dramas not only the deteriorating and destructive nature of sin; he perceived another principle working, the same that attracted Saint Paul: that where sin abounds the forces of good are released to overcome the evil.

These plays also discover to us the kind of man the poet admired. There is a general agreement among students of Shakespeare that Henry V, brave in battle, calm in disaster, victorious against heavy odds through superior valor of soul, democratic in his sympathies, just in judgment and deed, is the poet's hero among men of affairs. Such a man has strength because he rests on eternal verities. Good-will, courage, magnanimity, honor — such virtues are royal, and work well in the battle of life wherever one's field may be.

He puts in the mouth of Henry V a belief which seems

to have been fundamental with him, for he expresses it in many forms, and makes it determine the development of many a plot. It is this:

> There is some soul of goodness in things evil
> Would men observingly distil it out.

THE SONNETS

About 1594 Shakespeare made test of his poetic powers in sonnet form, a literary convention then enjoying large popularity. These sonnets are arranged in a sequence, one hundred and fifty-four in all. The first one hundred and twenty-six are addressed to a youth of compelling beauty; the remainder are written to a woman whose influence over the poet appears to have been malign. To what extent they reveal actual experience is a matter of debate. That their formative and pervading spirit discloses the poet's real self may be assumed. They show him to have been, as Professor Dowden suggests, much of a Romeo and something of a Hamlet, keenly sensitive both to love and injury, yet capable of generous forgiveness. Here, as well as in his plays, there is not a single 'cold-blooded, hard, or selfish line.' He may have been using the literary fashion of the period, but it is not difficult to discern in some of the sonnets Shakespeare's real self speaking in all sincerity. He had his moments of disillusionment:

> When, in disgrace with Fortune and men's eyes,
> I all alone beweep my outcast state,

And trouble deaf heaven with my bootless cries,
And look upon myself and curse my fate,
Wishing me like to one more rich in hope,
Featur'd like him, like him with friends possess'd,
Desiring this man's art, and that man's scope,
With what I most enjoy contented least;

.   .   .   .

At times he had distaste with the actor's art:

Alas, 'tis true I have gone here and there,
And made myself a motley to the view,
Gored mine own thoughts, sold cheap what is most dear,
Made old offences of affections new;
Most true it is that I have look'd on truth
Askance and strangely....

But love, not self-pity, is the prevailing note, and his
preoccupation with love brings him face to face with
some very serious questions regarding the meaning of
life. Professor George Herbert Palmer, in his Ingersoll
Lecture on 'Intimations of Immortality in Shakespeare,'
traces the progress of these meditations most convincingly.
Out of the poet's love for a wonderful youth comes the
distressing thought that this beauty 'among the wastes
of time must go,' and be lost forever. Love and beauty
are so valuable, yet how transitory! Is there not some
antidote to cure the ravages of 'Time's injurious hand?'
This problem of overcoming the tyranny of Time Professor Palmer finds to be the groundwork of the sonnets.
The first seventeen play about the thought that the boy's
beauty will reappear in his descendants. But this is small
comfort, for the youth himself does not survive. In the
second group of one hundred and nine the poet advances

to the idea that he will confer an ideal immortality on the youth through his verses:

> Not marble, nor the gilded monuments
> Of princes, shall outlive this powerful rhyme.

And again,

> His beauty shall in these black lines be seen,
> And they shall live, and he in them still green.

Shakespeare lingers long on this thought, but it gives little comfort. Even though the memory of him survives, the youth dies.

In the final section the author represents himself as falling under the spell of a dark enchantress. The one hundred and twenty-ninth sonnet describes his shame that he has walked in the path which leads to hell. The good in him rebels fiercely against the lustful passions which have dominated him. But they are not his true self. In sonnet one hundred and forty-six he bursts forth in a forcible assertion of the soul's victory over the 'rebel powers' within it:

> Poor soul, the centre of my sinful earth,
> Fool'd by these rebel powers that thee array,
> Why dost thou pine within and suffer dearth,
> Painting thy outward walls so costly gay?
> Why so large cost, having so short a lease,
> Dost thou upon thy fading mansion spend?
> Shall worms, inheritors of this excess,
> Eat up thy charge? Is this thy body's end?
> Then, soul, live thou upon thy servant's loss,
> And let that pine to aggravate thy store;
> Buy terms divine by selling hours of dross;
> Within be fed, without be rich no more.
> So shalt thou feed on Death, that feeds on men,
> And Death once dead, there's no more dying then.

Professor Palmer makes no claim that Shakespeare is consciously recording three stages of a larger hope, immortality through breed, memory, personal survival. All the more significant is it that in dealing with concrete experiences he is forced to look on individual immortality and find it a refuge.

What I would call to the reader's attention is the fact that in the sonnets Shakespeare presents an intuition which reappears in increasing frequency in his dramas, until in those of the final period it becomes a dominant force, a pervading glory. It is a penetration to something in our humanity which is superior to disaster, the changes of time, and the wrath of evil enemies; something spiritual that feeds on death and tribulation. This fact that hostile forces may be so confronted and subdued by the moral will that one is ennobled by the bitter experience finds fitting expression in the one hundred and nineteenth sonnet:

> O benefit of ill! now I find true
> That better is by evil still made better;
> And ruin'd love, when it is built anew,
> Grows fairer than at first, more strong, far greater.

This is not a passing fancy; it is a truth, a process, which Shakespeare used to transform his latter plays from tragedy to comedy — comedy in Dante's meaning. Here is an addition to the thought of the Greek dramatists that wisdom comes through suffering. Shakespeare broadens wisdom to include vitality and transcendency of character. Conflict with evil not only teaches one something; it makes one something, more strong, far greater.

What wisdom and power came to him through his meditations on life in its darker aspects will be considered in our study of the tragedies.

The Period of Tragedy

After some ten years of successful presentation of life in comedy and history, Shakespeare definitely turned to tragedy. Some consider this change of mood a proof that he personally experienced years of bitter disillusionment; others see only a change of fashion in the plays demanded by the public; perhaps he was simply testing his genius in another field.

Whatever the impelling cause, the poet now lets his eager imagination go down into the depths that he may explore evil in its utmost horror, and grief in its utmost despair. It seems probable, however, that more than the dramatist's imagination was engaged. The amazing power he displayed must have come from the depths of his personality. The pulse of a real struggle with evil in himself and in the world beats in these pages. He is now in middle life, being about thirty-six years of age. The glamour which a youthful spirit casts over the world has vanished; his maturer mind faces grim reality and asks the inevitable questions. That spot midway in the journey of our life is a perilous place for most of us. The visions of youth have lost their brightness and fade into the light of common day. If one has sufficient wisdom and valor to reaffirm his devotion to the glory and the gleam, he wins a most important victory. If, however, the Great Distaste lays hold of him and conquers, then the rest of the journey lies through the bitter land of cynicism and futility. To this critical time Shakespeare has now come. The days of his youth and apprenticeship are over. He is too great a man to dwell continuously on the lighter aspects of life. Dante at thirty-five met a similar crisis and descended into hell to explore the nature and results of evil. Shakespeare is now in the fullness of his power. Minute observation, profound thought, imaginative sympathy have ripened into intuition. Knowledge has become wisdom, and reasoning gives place to insight. Also he has attained superlative mastery over words and can use them as obedient servants for the full utterance of his thoughts.

The time of the tragedies stretches through the years between 1599 and 1609. The comedies, written at the beginning of this period, have lost their merry laughter, and have much bitterness. In the historical plays which draw their plots from Rome and Athens — *Julius Caesar, Antony and Cleopatra, Coriolanus, Timon of Athens* — we find a change of center. He is not concerned with representing truthfully the atmosphere, the contending principles, the social problems of the epochs chosen; character and passion are the dominant interest. He is less engaged with the qualities making for success or failure, and fixes his mind on the destiny of individuals as it is influenced by their ambitions, lusts, and undisciplined emotions.

Julius Caesar: *Impractical Idealism*

When Shakespeare turned for a theme to Roman history, the splendor of Caesar's career and the pity of his fate would immediately confront him. Perhaps his original purpose had been to make Caesar the hero of the play which bears his name. But the admirer of Henry V and the future creator of Prospero would surely be drawn to the moral grandeur of Brutus. His fate would seem more tragic than that of Caesar and its causes would engage the poet's far-searching curiosity. Although he closely follows the story as told by Plutarch, his own spiritual bent is clearly seen in his handling of the material.

Brutus, as Shakespeare conceives him, fails because with all his lofty idealism he lacks a sense of fact. His very nobility is his undoing, causing him to spare the life of Antony and generously allow him to speak at Caesar's funeral. His devotion to theories leads him to overrule Cassius, whose knowledge of existing situations is more accurate. In this rough world he suffered defeat, yet he remains the hero of the play, not his victorious rivals, not Caesar, not Antony. 'This is the noblest Roman of them all.' As Shakespeare brooded over the character and career of this Roman, he perceived in the austere moral sublimity of Brutus something of greater value than success in worldly affairs. Therefore after his defeat at Philippi he makes Brutus exclaim:

> I found no man but he was true to me.
> I shall have glory by this losing day,
> More than Octavius and Mark Antony
> By this vile conquest shall attain unto.

168

Character has its victories no less than war. Here again Shakespeare strikes the note which we heard in the sonnets and in the earlier plays. There is a greatness in the human spirit that rises superior to disaster, and is never so triumphant as in defeat. Out of disaster the larger good may be born.

> There is some soul of goodness in things evil,
> Would men observingly distil it out.
>
> .   .   .   .
>
> O benefit of ill! Now I find true
> That better is by evil still made better.

As the final curtain falls on the play, one has a distinct feeling of elation. He has been uplifted by the stately march of the verse, he has felt anew in Portia's fidelity the enchantment which the dramatist never fails to cast over the finest traits of womanhood; in Brutus he has perceived once more in moral heroism a virtue superior to the changing fortunes of the day.

Perhaps one's profoundest impression will be that we have not seen all when we have beheld men's deeds and have learned their motives. One has a sense of an Invisible Actor who is the Master of the Play, who works in strange, relentless ways to avenge the wrong and reveal the good. The Unseen Powers appear to be unfriendly to the baser actions of men. Blood drops from heaven, and ghostly warriors fight in the air. A purpose is working through the shifting deeds of men. A close-linked chain binds events together. 'Philippi ends what the Ides of

March began.' As the battle goes against him, Brutus exclaims:

> O Julius Caesar, thou art mighty yet!
> Thy spirit walks abroad, and turns our swords
> In our own proper entrails.

It is curious how this idea that wrong must be expiated crops out constantly in literature. It is a conviction laid down by long and hard experience. Brutus felt that his death was a genuine atonement for his mistakes, and exclaimed as he fell on his sword, 'Caesar, now be still.'

HAMLET: *The Coil of Destiny*

Had the dramatist's main interest been in producing a series of acceptable plays, he would naturally have followed *Julius Caesar* with *Antony and Cleopatra*. Being a poet as well as a playwright, his mind was engrossed in understanding the tragic experiences of men whose characters awaken one's admiration. Like Brutus, Hamlet is an arresting figure for his talents, his struggles, his fate.

The story of Amleth, or Hamlet, Prince of Denmark, had been a hero-tale in Europe since the twelfth century, when Saxo Grammaticus told of the tragic experiences of a Danish prince whose uncle had killed his father and married the Queen, had endeavored to entrap the prince by means of an eavesdropper and a young girl, had sent him to England with secret instructions that he be put to death. Amleth feigns madness, kills the usurper, persuades the people that he has acted justly, and is made king. This is a good story, so full of human interest that it became a legend and was told in tale and play in many forms. Shakespeare was attracted by the dramatic possibilities of the saga, but his imagination moved straight toward the psychological problems of such a character. What would be the doubts, the agony, the inhibitions of a noble-minded, sensitive man caught in such a network of intrigue? The poet evidently brooded long over the enigma, and so intensely realized the character, and put himself so completely in the place of the prince, that Hamlet grew to be very much like Shakespeare. This ancient story of lust and blood became under his treatment an open door into the depths of the soul, revealing the Everlasting working his resistless will.

No play that has ever been read or acted is so fertile in problems as this. Some scholars deny that there is any problem at all. There would be no play, they declare, if there were no delays between the murder and the revenge; to many it is the tragedy of an upright, introspective, vacillating intellect forced by necessity to decisive action; to others it is Shakespeare's interpretation of the irresolution of Essex. Into these many and engrossing questions we shall not go. The labyrinth is so intricate that even the archangels of scholarship tread cautiously and fail to agree on a common path.

For our purpose it is sufficient for us to remember that the play was written for a theater audience. It was written to give them pleasure and to express a phase of life which seemed to the great dramatist to be important.

He must do this in a way which should not do violence to their instincts and beliefs or to his own. Doubtless the attentive reader, pondering the marvelous sentences, will find many subtle problems of extreme interest suggested. But Shakespeare was too skilled an artist not to make the main lines of his thought evident to the mind of the average spectator. Also we may remember that the meaning of a work of art is not confined to the purpose of the artist; its final value is its effect on the beholder! Its permanent worth is in the stamp it leaves on the generations of men. Tragedy to be great must purge and elevate the spirit of the audience.

We turn our attention therefore to the question, what does this tremendous drama do to sharpen our insight into the mysteries of life and to cleanse and ennoble our emotions?

My own impressions of the meaning of the play were formed under the most favorable circumstances. In the first stage production which I attended Edwin Booth was the interpreter of the melancholy Dane. The sad, graceful figure, clothed in dark velvet, the black hair, the glowing eyes, the compelling magic of that marvelous voice, all served to quicken in one the sense of the mystery encompassing the world and the tangled ways of men. The opening challenge, 'Who's there?' is a question sent into the darkness, suggestive of clashing forces, fear, and mystery. It is the keynote of all that follows. Throughout the drama one feels the presence of a Disposer of events, a Power not ourselves working his high purpose. And something better further on for the tortured soul of Hamlet is intimated in that prayer of Horatio, uttered so spontaneously out of the emotions aroused by the fated climax:

> Good night, sweet prince;
> And flights of angels sing thee to thy rest!

The tragedy begins with a question hurled into the dark; it ends with a sense of a heaven of ministering angels and of eternal peace.

Throughout the play the spectator feels the constant presence of a power working to destroy evil and establish the good. Six times seeming accidents turn out to be links in a chain of punishment. As Mr. A. C. Bradley so justly observes, the effect of these accidents is 'to strengthen in the spectator the feeling that, whatever may become of Hamlet, and whether he wills it or not, his task will surely be accomplished, because it is the purpose of a power against which both he and his enemy are impotent, and which makes them the instruments of its own will.' Hamlet himself is represented as having a strong conviction of a providential ordering of events. This would be natural for him because of the times and his hereditary belief. But he asserts this belief with a frequency and an emphasis which issue from deep conviction, formed out of personal experience, and Shakespeare, living imaginatively in Hamlet, utters the faith arising naturally out of the crisis and its closely fitted events. He unhesitatingly uses the language habitual to religion, and he uses it with a subtle discrimination which shows long meditation on these mysteries. Hamlet repeatedly affirms that he is conscious of Another working through him, even through his mistakes.

> Our indiscretion sometimes serves us well,
> When our deep plots do pall; and that should teach us
> There's a divinity that shapes our ends,
> Rough-hew them how we will.

Again how nicely he makes the player-king discern between man's conscious freedom and the purpose working through him:

> Our thoughts are ours, their ends none of our own.

When he needs a seal to stamp with authority his letter to the English king, in what men call chance he sees a providential prevision,

> ...in that was Heaven ordinant.
> I had my father's signet in my purse.

As he goes to the fatal duel he comforts himself with the thought, 'There's a special providence in the fall of a sparrow.' He assumes throughout the play what is ordained will come; 'the readiness is all.'

The belief in the providential ordering of events was the common faith of the time. Shakespeare in making his audience and readers vividly aware of the accepted belief was doing more than confirming it; he was disclosing his own conviction that retributive justice is the controlling law of tragic art. He wrote good tragedy because he was true to the sovereign laws of the world and to the deepest instincts of the soul of man. Claudius seemed so undiscoverable when he did the deed. No eye saw him, no ear heard him, and apparently a heedless universe permitted his plans to prosper. Evil had been done, and the Eternal cared not. But the dead had risen to tell the dreadful secret; the guilty conscience of the King had betrayed him; the avenging forces which punish the sins of men had moved slowly, but surely. The King's plot miscarries, the pirate ship brings Hamlet back to Denmark, Laertes' better nature interferes with his skillful sword, the rapiers are changed, the Queen drinks the poisoned cup, the King's guilt becomes manifest to all the world. Hamlet, with untainted mind, may now send his dagger to the King's heart. The total impression is of the moral framework of the world, of a law that is not mocked, neither does it slumber.

How closely Hamlet's destiny was bound up in his character has often been remarked. Othello's simple mind would have been unvisited by such scruples or such hesitation. He would have run his sword through the King in instant revenge. And Hamlet likewise would not have been an easy prey to Iago.

To the nature and sufferings of Hamlet Shakespeare had given prolonged attention. There is evidence that he expended painstaking care over both structure and thought. If he had been intent upon writing a play which would leave his audience in a pleasant frame of mind he would have followed the ancient tradition and let Hamlet be crowned and victorious over his enemies. But one of Shakespeare's most characteristic traits was the intensity with which he followed the close-linked chain of moral causes and effects. Hamlet had lived too deeply into the suffering and mystery of life to permit so facile a solution of his problem. He must drink the cup to the dregs. Evil is not so light a thing. When the curtain falls on this drama with Hamlet, the King, the Queen and Laertes dead upon the stage, the memory still fresh of Ophelia's suicide, Polonius slain, the Ghost revealing the secret deed which caused all the destruction, the spectator is in no mood to discredit the moral law. He feels that Nemesis is no poetic imagination. The little writers often make lust appear glamorous, and unscrupulous ambition an admirable exhibition of virility, but never the great poets. These do not find that poetic justice is inevitable in this strange universe, but they discover that all deeds are fertile and bring forth a harvest, even a hundred fold.

The catastrophe which ends the drama of Hamlet, the stage thick with dead, some innocent, some damned in guilt, is thoroughly representative of Shakespeare's method: an evil deed multiplies itself. Once launched in this closely woven system of things, it goes beyond the purpose of the perpetrator and spreads devastation far and wide.

Shakespeare in his other great tragedies — *Julius Caesar, Othello, Macbeth, Lear* — is satisfied to end the story in the death of the hero who has paid with his life for his sin or his weakness, and the audience finds repose in death's mystery and solemn peace. But in this drama there is an intimation of life beyond death, a compensation more abundant than repose. The heart that has been cracked by the guilt of others would seem to deserve more than the escape from his enemies through the gates of death. And Shakespeare living in Hamlet has confronted one after another the darkest mysteries which appall the human mind; now when he comes to the last and greatest

176

his imagination follows his hero into the shadows and intimates that Heavenly powers offer triumph to the brave spirit whom earth has broken.

> Good night, sweet prince;
> And flights of angels sing thee to thy rest.

OTHELLO: *A Presentation of Moral Evil*

In this drama the tragic collision is not within the hero's own breast, nor in his struggle with untoward conditions. Here we have a clash of personalities, a net woven by human intrigue rather than by a watchful Providence. The noble simplicity of Othello is sport to the cunning malignity of Iago. The alert mind of Hamlet would easily have detected the ancient's villainous designs. The tragedy lies in the fact that two such natures should come together under such conditions.

The plot and its development so evidently has its origin and direction in Iago's own scheming brain that the key to the tragedy is in his character. Our thoughts are turned in this drama to the enigma of human depravity, not to the mystery of the ways of God. As Mr. A. C. Bradley in his great work, *Shakespearian Tragedy*, truly says, 'We seem to be aware in it [*Othello*] of certain limitations, a partial suppression of that element in Shakespeare's mind which unites him with the mystical poets and with the great musicians and philosophers.' And again, 'This play does not dilate the imagination by vague suggestions of huge universal powers working in the world of individual fate and passion.' Our confidence that Iago's intrigues will be frustrated grows out of our inherited instinct that the cunning are caught in their own craftiness, rather than in glimpses given to us of a Power which entangles the wise in their own conceit.

In Brutus, Shakespeare had studied the mistakes of a good man; in Iago he ponders the ways and the character of cold-blooded, calculating villainy.

When this treacherous reptile first appears, he is represented as one who is generally trusted by his intimates, especially for his honesty and fidelity. We infer that his previous life had been respectable, self-interest having kept him within the decencies of convention. He is respected because no severe temptation has aroused the fiend within him to break forth destructively.

When the play opens his self-esteem has recently been wounded, for Cassio has been preferred before him as chief lieutenant. This makes him hate the Moor. Moreover, Othello's unbending integrity would be a constant rebuke to Iago's shifty morals, and the general's more ponderous mind would irk the ancient's nimble wit. Iago confesses that he serves Othello only 'in the form and visages of duty':

> Though I do hate him as I do hell-pains,
> Yet, for necessity of present life,
> I must show out a flag and sign of love.

In the original story which Shakespeare used as the basis of this drama, Iago's motive was love for Desdemona. In the present play lust occupies a very subordinate position, Shakespeare choosing to portray a villain who is a man of intellect and will, rather than a man of passion. His devilishness draws from deeper fountains than the flesh. What makes him the evil thing he is, eager to ensnare Othello body and soul, is his utter egotism. 'I follow but myself,' he confesses. Although he has lived four times seven years, yet he affirms, 'I never found a man who knew how to love himself.' Plainly he intends to be governed in the future by absolute egoism. He will love himself, and in no vulgar way, but artistically, in a manner befitting a man of his intellectual resources. Heretofore he has restrained his self-centering passions; now he is determined to give them free play, and his excuse is his secret hatred of the Moor.

Most of the reasons he gives for his conduct are but an attempt to rationalize his malignity. As others have pointed out, the force which drives him and holds him steadily and relentlessly to his cruel intrigue is his desire to assert his superiority over those whose virtue makes his character seem shabby, and whose position outranks his own.

Iago is not only utterly self-centered; he naturally gravitates to the lowest, whether he interprets words, motives, or character. Yet, strangely enough, to the nobility of Othello and the virtue of Desdemona he does full homage. This honor will prove their undoing.

> So will I turn her virtue into pitch,
> And out of her own goodness make the net
> That shall enmesh them all.

Then in cold blood, with will wholly bent on evil, using subtlest skill and devilish ingenuity he weaves his net about his victims.

Such is the man Shakespeare created as a fitting personification of moral evil. Not a bestial creature of fleshly passions, not a low-browed brute dominated by hate and greed, but a respectable gentleman, conspicuously trusted for his honesty, vividly conscious of intellectual superiority, served by a will, daring in action, and cooled to patience. Because of his own inordinate self-esteem he holds all men in contempt, and judges grossly every motive and character. In the presence of the good he is uncomfortable. What would give such a man the greatest satisfaction? Certainly the mastery over his betters.

But he will gain his ends artistically, in a manner that will both demonstrate his superiority and enhance his self-esteem. He would treat Othello as Brutus would Caesar:

> Let's carve him as a dish fit for the gods,
> Not hew him as a carcass fit for hounds.

The more difficult the task, the greater the artist's enjoyment. To weave an intricate net about a despised victim, this, to a malicious and resourceful mind, is joy, this is ecstasy.

Notice how Shakespeare in his portrayal of Iago reaffirms the ancient teaching of the Church that the essence of sin is some form of selfishness. The solar system works harmoniously because each planet revolves in its proper orbit around the central sun. Let Jupiter determine to be the center, and there would follow 'the wreck of matter and the crush of worlds.' The theologians and the poets are agreed that the dominant cause of human ill grows out of the fact that the individual asserts his central importance and would make God and his fellow man revolve about him. Dante represents pride as the most fundamental of mortal sins; Milton ascribes the woe of the world to the ambition of Satan to occupy the throne of the Almighty. The Devil in popular tradition, and in the poets from Job to Goethe, is not a monster of brutish passions; he companions with the sons of God, is incredibly clever, plausible, and persistent. At first he succeeds, yet in the end he fails because, after all, Job does serve God for naught, and the soul of Faust has depths of which Mephistopheles is ignorant, and Iago's fabrication of lies is shattered by a loyalty upon which he had not reckoned.

Shakespeare in his presentation of moral evil is in the great tradition: the hypocrite is farther from the kingdom of God than the harlot. Intellect and volition divorced from human kindness are blind, destructive, and foolish, 'more fell than anguish, hunger, or the sea.'

It is recognized that the tragedy of *Othello*, chiefly concerned as it is with the clash of two opposite characters, does not give one the same sense of supernatural powers working through human destiny that we find in the other tragedies. But the moral structure of life is recognized, if not in its grandeur, yet in its precision. At first all chance and fortune work for the success of Iago's plans; he grows in confidence, his purpose becomes an infatuation, and he is carried by the current of events resistlessly to his doom. Then in a moment a few words from his wife reveal his hideous villainy. The sheer goodness of Desdemona has aroused a saving loyalty in the soul of Emilia, and Iago is exposed. The blindness of evil to the reserves of the good has ever proved its undoing. The inherent decency of the nature of things now thrusts Iago aside as a very slight thing. Quick death would be inadequate punishment for a villain who had worked so great destruction. Dramatic art, and a deep instinct in both the dramatist and his audience, would be violated unless Iago more fully expiated his fiendish crimes. The tragic mood and ancient wisdom will be content with nothing less.

> To you, lord governor,
> Remains the censure of this hellish villain,
> The time, the place, the torture, O, *enforce* it!

There are three other personifications of moral evil in the literature of western civilization — Dante's Lucifer, Milton's Satan, and Goethe's Mephistopheles. How different they are! Milton's Satan is of heroic proportions, an archangel dimmed of his primal luster, like a sun shining through a mist, capable of challenging the supremacy of Heaven's Eternal King. Damned, but glorious.

Mephistopheles is very much like Iago, a modern gentleman, of excellent address, most practical intelligence, and astonishing abilities. But he fails of his object because there is in Faust a spiritual nature whose necessities and aspirations he fails to comprehend. He and Iago fail from the same defect — spiritual blindness.

182

Dante's Lucifer is a personification of evil in its ultimate character. It is grotesque, self-destructive, sodden in insensibility.

These master-poets differ, for they are painting the same subject from different points of view. Milton shows sin at the beginning, when it appears glorious and attractive; Shakespeare and Goethe treat it as it appears today — a very human thing, plausible, adroit, not altogether abhorrent, yet overreaching itself through spiritual blindness. Dante is interested in its ultimate nature and consequences, when it shows itself to be foul, miserable, foolish, utterly without attraction.

MACBETH: *The Law Within*

Two things fill my soul with always new and ever-increasing wonder and awe, and often and persistently my thought busies itself therewith — the starry heavens above me and the moral law within me. KANT.

In his meditations on the forces whose collision makes up life's tragedy, Shakespeare could not escape the study of a guilty conscience. Its dramatic possibilities were too great, its significance too profound.

The condition of the times doubtless had much to do with the selection of the subject. James VI of Scotland had on July 25, 1603, been crowned James I of England. The court players would not unnaturally turn their thoughts to a plot having some connection with the new monarch. Shakespeare took up his Holinshed and found there the story of 'one Macbeth, a valiant gentleman, and one that, if he had not been somewhat cruel of nature, might have been thought most worthy the government of a realm.' Walking one day with Banquo, after their return from warring against the Danes, they met 'three women in strange and wild apparel, resembling the creatures of the elder world.' One of them cried out, 'All hail, Macbeth, thane of Glamis!' The second cried, 'Hail, Macbeth, thane of Cawdor!' And the third, 'All hail, Macbeth, that hereafter shall be king of Scotland!' After the first two prophecies had been fulfilled, 'Macbeth, revolving the thing in his mind, began even then to devise how he might attain to the kingdom . . . but especially his wife lay sore upon him to attempt the thing, as she was very ambitious, burning in unquenchable desire to bear the name of a queen.' As Banquo was the traditional ancestor of the house of Stuart, and the accession of Malcolm was important to the future relationship of the Celt and the Saxon, the play was appropriate for the time and for the state of the dramatist's mind. After the treatment of the cold-blooded malignity of Iago, this legend suggested a presentation of evil as it runs its devastating course through the conscience and character of a brave, imaginative, honorably disposed man whose ambitions battled with his better nature. Lady Macbeth would also interest him. Hitherto most of his female characters have been alluring; now he will understand woman unsexed, demonized.

Shakespeare has written no sublimer tragedy. His central figures are of heroic proportions; the atmosphere is one of blackness, foreboding, and terror. Most of the scenes take place in the night, the time when ghosts do stalk abroad, when guilty consciences awake, and superstition is too powerful to be restrained by common sense. Blood and visionary daggers, calling voices, clutching hands, and prayers that stick in the throat, all add to the horror. So concentrated is the passion, so intense and sustained the imagination, that Mr. Masefield claims that half of the tragedy must have been written at a sitting. Certainly Shakespeare was in the Great Mood that day. His imagination must have been expanded and aflame to clothe thought in imagery like this:

> ... his virtues
> Will plead like angels, trumpet-tongued, against
> The deep damnation of his taking-off;
> And pity, like a naked new-born babe
> Striding the blast, or heaven's cherubin hors'd
> Upon the sightless couriers of the air,
> Shall blow the horrid deed in every eye,
> That tears shall drown the wind....

Not since Aeschylus put his Furies on the stage had dramatic genius visualized the secret workings of the conscience so startlingly, so sublimely. Yet the Greek falls far short of the English poet in subtlety of analysis.

Macbeth is the dramatization of Shakespeare's brooding thoughts on the workings of a guilty conscience as it effects two contrasted temperaments. The material which he found in the chronicles he uses freely to fit the problem in his mind. The sin is vaulting ambition which o'erleaps itself, 'catches the nearest way' to reach the desired end, willfully violates sacred and accepted obligations, thus bringing upon itself the retributive penalties of an outraged conscience and enmeshing the victim in conditions which force him to multiplied horrors.

Shakespeare set himself to his task, not as a moral teacher imposing a theory, but as an artist who delights to trace the effects of deeds on the character and destinies of men, and as a dramatist who would present them most powerfully. In this study of moral evil, Shakespeare has an advantage not possessed by Greek tragedy. The ancients because of their theories of the unities of time and place could not with equal clearness show a character gradually deteriorating. This the larger freedom enjoyed by the Elizabethan drama permitted. .

The hero is presented in the first scene as a man of honor, worthy of the esteem in which he was held by his peers. To Lady Macbeth he seems to be,

> . . . too full o' the milk of human kindness
> To catch the nearest way. Thou wouldst be great,
> Art not without ambition, but without
> The illness should attend it; what thou wouldst highly,
> That wouldst thou holily; wouldst not play false,
> And yet wouldst wrongly win. . . .

That is, he is a man disquieted by moral ideas, not governed by them to his own disadvantage. His imagination is so closely allied to his finer sentiments that he cannot, like Iago, enjoy his villainy. Immediately after the treacherous act his sensitive mind envisages the consequences. He knows that the evil deed is not the be-all and the end-all, and that even-handed justice will hold the poisoned chalice to his lips.

No sooner has the fatal blow been struck than instantly he is aware of those energies in the soul and about it which attend on evil. He hears voices, he cannot pray, the knocking at the door fills him with terror. Most insistent of all is his conviction that he can sleep no more, and that great Neptune's ocean could not wash the blood clean from his hand. But retributive justice is not satisfied with the lashes inflicted by conscience. The first bloody deed leads to others. To secure the results of his first murder he is driven to wade still deeper in blood. Banquo must be put out of the way; neither must his line inherit the reward of Macbeth's valor. This murder but increases his unrest. Terrible dreams shake him nightly, and in his waking thoughts, his victims seem more fortunate than he. They at least have peace:

> ... Duncan is in his grave;
> After life's fitful fever he sleeps well.

Not only is sleep banished from his eyes, the meaning passes out of life:

> There's nothing serious in mortality.
> All is but toys: renown and grace is dead;
> The wine of life is drawn, and the mere lees
> Is left this vault to brag of.

Most memorable of all are these words of utter disillusion:

> Tomorrow, and tomorrow, and tomorrow,
> Creeps in this petty pace from day to day
> To the last syllable of recorded time;
> And all our yesterdays have lighted fools
> The way to dusty death. Out, out, brief candle!
> Life's but a walking shadow; a poor player
> That struts and frets his hour upon the stage
> And then is heard no more. It is a tale
> Told by an idiot, full of sound and fury,
> Signifying nothing.

His fear drives him to desperation and further murders; 'each new morn more widows howl.' As he cannot draw strength from the resources of his moral integrity and a just cause, he is plunged deeper into superstition, and learns how deceitful are the promises of evil: they keep the word of promise to the ear and break it to the hope.

The end of it all is his bloody head held in the hand of Macduff, whom he had most wronged. Thus is the old wisdom vindicated; there is a way that seemeth good to a man, but the end thereof is death. The Unseen Powers do not forget, neither are they indifferent.

In Lady Macbeth Shakespeare shows the same ambition and the same guilt working in a different nature. At the beginning of the play she is the dominant figure, but the King's heart hardens into reckless courage as difficulties throng upon him. She breaks under the burden. Awake, she is able to control her thoughts, but when the will is asleep the horror possesses her until she seeks refuge in suicide. She is a frailer creature than Clytemnestra.

Macbeth is the most vivid and impressive presentation of remorse to be found in literature. Neither in hell nor in purgatory did Dante look upon torment of like character and intensity.

Remorse — *remordere*, the rebite of sin — is an ever-recurring theme with Shakespeare. Twelve years before in *Richard III* great tragedy had centered around this conviction; it is part of the providential order in *Hamlet*, and in *Macbeth* it is truth lighted with undying fire. Let the reader not fail to mark the distinction between the poignant sense of sin which visits the holiest saints, and remorse, the rebite of sin, through memory and reason, when one keeps the reward and the evil purpose with no bent toward contrition and restitution.

KING LEAR: *A Study in Inhumanity*

In his interest in character, and his eagerness to understand this human drama in which all men and women are players, Shakespeare has been meditating evil and its tragic consequences in many forms. Now, in the words of Mr. Dover Wilson, he girds himself for 'one of the most perilous and arduous adventures ever undertaken by the spirit of man.' He will go to the depths of human depravity and explore its capacity for torment and disgust. The result will be 'the greatest monument of human misery and despair in the literature of the world.'

Dante found the lowest hell to be a zone of ice where traitors to friends and kindred existed in frozen isolation. Those deepest damned had severed all the ties binding them to their fellows, and inevitably the kindly currents of their natures had congealed. Through spiritual insensibility they had become benumbed and brutish. The lowest hell into which the human soul can descend is not a condition hot with the fires of remorse, but one frigid with inhumanity. Into this arctic selfishness the imagination of Shakespeare now enters.

He constructs his characters to develop his thought and to make clear his conclusions. Lear is a willful and violent old man who will brook no crossing of his whims. His two eldest daughters, Goneril and Regan, having received a kingdom from their father, ungratefully thrust him from their homes into the unpitying storm and to madness. Their love is lust, and in every relationship they are false.

Gloucester is as unreasonable and testy as Lear. Edmund is the kind of villain who would have admired Iago.

If Shakespeare paints evil in its most fiendish form in his bad characters, he represents his good characters as incredibly loyal and self-sacrificing. Extreme stands in contrast to extreme. One is reminded of the war in heaven; devils and angels are here in conflict.

When the final curtain falls the issue seems undecided. Lear has found that which his heart most craved — the perfect love of Cordelia. But at the very moment of reconciliation one dies of strangling and the other of a broken heart. Malignity has after all struck the last blow.

The fitness of this tragic ending has been the cause of much discussion. Early audiences found it so distressing that Nahum Tate rewrote it, marrying Edgar to Cordelia, in whose home Lear lived in peace. For one hundred and fifty years the play was thus rendered, until in 1838 Macready produced the whole as Shakespeare had written it, and gave to the world the poet's thought as he had fashioned it.

The long ranges of experience bear solemn witness that the overwhelming of the good by the evil is one of the tragic aspects of life. Of this Calvary is the eternal reminder. If the poet follows human misery to the bounds of mortal wisdom, he will find few happy endings, few satisfactory reconciliations. Nothing is finished. He confronts the Infinite Mystery and the curtain falls, not upon an explanation, but upon a summons to high faith. Shakespeare was as powerless as the rest of us to solve the riddle of the universe. In this tragedy he discloses the one view of Providence which is true to the deeper phases of suffering — true both to our experience and our needs. We know that the compensating balance is not struck in the short compass of our earthly existence. That it is struck at all is an act of heroic trust. As the poet could not truthfully portray such bitter wrongs to be easily atoned by a short period of uncertain happiness, he lays the problems of reconciliation, only partly solved, in the presence of the Eternal.

Not only are the deaths of Cordelia and Lear true to large areas of mortal experience; they are dramatically necessary. The measure of great tragedy is its power to elevate the spirit of the spectator to awe and pity, thus purging it of lesser feelings. This can be done only as the conclusion leaves the spectator in a mood of solemn reconciliation. All the great dramatists have found that the death of the heroic victim has this effect. It is comparatively easy to tie the threads of life into hard knots, but difficult to untie them to the satisfaction of the spectator. The dramatist finds his severest test in the final scene when the turbulent passions of the audience must be reconciled. The happy ending is too superficial and improbable; therefore death has been seized upon as the instrument most potent. The villain's death seems the natural consummation of his crimes; the hero's death is not his defeat, but his escape. He is set free from the toils of his enemies.

After these voices there is peace. He has become superior to the world and all its clamor and malignity. Repose is as essential to great tragedy as struggle, and of this perfect repose death is an effective symbol; it suggests permanence and finality which a few days of happiness could not assure.

As he went through this hell of inhumanity, Shakespeare, like Dante, tells what he found there of truth and value. Prominently, at the very opening, through the misfortunes of Lear and Gloucester, he teaches the ancient maxim of the Greeks, 'Naught in excess.' Violent willfulness, untempered passion bring the inevitable reaction. He also fully accords with them in revealing that wisdom comes through suffering. By his agonies Lear learned patience, sympathy with others, self-renunciation, thus saving his own soul. At the end Lear, the violent, has become like Edgar, 'pregnant to good pity, by the art of known and feeling sorrows.' Shakespeare worked on the principle that the instincts and experience of men show that the universe works for spiritual valor and steadfast faith. The evildoer is caught in his own net:

> The gods are just, and of our pleasant vices
> Make instruments to plague us.

But their justice, be it noted, is not even-handed requital — it is in the sure connection of a deed with its consequence. Whatsoever a man soweth that shall he also reap. In Cordelia's death Shakespeare reminds us that prosperity is not the inevitable reward of virtue. Not on ease and abundant possessions do the gods throw incense, but on that integrity of soul which is faithful to the end.

The most lasting impression, I think, which this study of the depths of man's inhumanity to man conveys to the reader is not how far men descend in the depths of depravity, but how great nobility is in them. Through what untold distress will they maintain their hold on loyalty! How lavishly they give all for love! What will they not hazard for honor! I do not believe that Shakespeare laid down his pen, as some writers affirm, 'as cynical as Iago and as disillusioned as Macbeth.' Rather he was confirmed in his conviction that in the mud and scum of things there are virtues of inestimable worth. 'No man,' says Sir Walter Raleigh, 'can explore the possibilities of evil as Shakespeare did without peril to his own soul.' But he found Cordelia as well as Goneril. His penetration of evil sustained his faith in the reality of virtue, radiant and unconquerable.

TIMON OF ATHENS

After *Lear* we have one other play expressive of the extreme tragic mood. *Timon of Athens* is only partly the work of Shakespeare, but in those portions which bear his magic charm Timon pours out the vials of his wrath upon the villainy of men with an intensity which some authorities think is the authentic voice of Shakespeare, and which shows him distraught to the verge of madness. But it is not necessary to put forth so drastic an explanation. Timon, like Lear, was a man of undisciplined passions. He lived, at the beginning, in a dream world in which men are friendly and open-handed. Trusting his fellows, he gave generously from his abundant wealth. With his fortune gone, his friends leave him, and he rages at the selfishness and base ingratitude of men. He is passion's slave and abandons himself to unbridled imprecations. He scorns the pleasanter ways of men. Timon has met the evil of the world and his personal wrongs without poise and without reason — angrily, bitterly, insanely. Therefore he reaps what he has sowed. He is not heroic enough to distill wisdom from suffering.

Tragedy as Revelation

When Shakespeare turned from comedy and historical drama to tragedy, he laid hold of the most potent instrument literature offers to reveal life in its depths of depravity and in its heights of moral excellency, for tragedy is 'a vision into the heart of life.'

The epic and the tragic drama are literature in its highest forms, yet they differ in the aspects of life which they envisage. The epic relates a series of adventures by a hero and therefore reflects life under many conditions; tragedy centers interest on one fateful deed, on one focal and tremendous moment when powerful passions disclose their nature and exert their strength.

Tragedy brings a deed and its consequences together; it presents the crucial moment when an action is known in the light of its results, and the unbreakable tie binding effect with cause is vividly realized. We feel intensely that there is no unrelated thing, we glimpse the framework of law in which all life is lived: we have our clearest insight into the capacity of human nature to endure and to transcend: we see truth, not in the abstractions of philosophy, but visibly in terms of human passions and suffering, when humanity is on the rack and makes its great confessions, and achieves its sublimest victories. In tragedy we are confronted by the great questions — of Fate and Providence, of Freedom and Destiny, of Love and Sin. Melodrama harrows our feelings without unveiling those deeper realities which sustain the spirit in its suffering and go far to explain the meaning of it. It lacks that solemn vision into the heart of life which by elevating our moods purifies our souls.

On the contrary, tragedy discovers the flaming walls of the world, the spiritual pattern believed in by the author, the audience, the actors. Great tragedy is successful and ennobling because it accords with our deep instincts, with racial experience, with our strong faith in what is, what may be, or what ought to be. The characters act and the plot unfolds conformably to the laws of nature and the structure of the human spirit. It not only discloses the laws of the spiritual world; it manifests the possible nobility of humanity. 'The powers of evil and horror,' says Gilbert Murray, 'must be granted their full scope; it is only thus that we triumph over them. Only when they have worked their uttermost will do we realize that there remains something in man's soul which is forever beyond their grasp and has power in its own right to make life beautiful.'

But having thus released the powers of evil, how can the dramatist close his play in a manner that will con-

vince him that he has been true to the strictest requirements of his theme, and compel the spectators to leave the
theater in that state of spiritual purification of which
Aristotle wrote? The termination of a play really expresses a dramatist's criticism of the universe. To represent the hero as ultimately successful and 'happy ever
after' is not usually a veracious or even a possible ending
of desperate spiritual struggle. Happiness is too imperma-
nent; it is not the inevitable reward of right doing.

Aeschylus ended the *Oresteia* with a scene of reconciliation. Sophocles represents Oedipus as learning wisdom
through suffering and receiving approving honors from the
gods. But often the struggle has been too terrible and
involved to be terminated either by compensation, vindication, or explanation. It is too recent to show the soul
of goodness in the evil thing, or the wisdom distilled
through agony.

Therefore the dramatist has recourse to death as the
chief reconciler, death with its mystery, its repose, its
suggestion of the eternal. The death of the villain accords
with our sense of justice, and even the death of the hero
relieves the strain, lifting us into the realm of peace, and
suggesting security from the shafts of hate.

> Duncan is in his grave;
> After life's fitful fever he sleeps well.
> Treason has done his worst: nor steel, nor poison,
> Malice domestic, foreign levy, nothing,
> Can touch him further.

The fact of death awes us; the eternal silence quiets our
questionings, and gives intimations of a higher tribunal.

Shakespeare closes all of his great tragedies with the death of the hero. But he does not leave the audience disillusioned and in distaste of life. The effect of great tragedy, as was said long ago, is purification. It stimulates our compassion, for we witness terrible agony; it fills us with awe by bringing us face to face with vast powers which are not of today or yesterday, but control the destinies of men in all generations; it girds us with spiritual strength because in entering sympathetically into suffering greater than our own we learn endurance; it reveals the heroic qualities in humanity which enable it to triumph over disaster; we learn that while outwardly all may be in ruins, inwardly all may be victory. The effect of great tragedy is not despair, but elevation; even evil is not irresponsible malignity, but is the servitor of law.

Reconciliation: The Period of Romance

For some ten years the imagination of Shakespeare had been living in the deep shadows of life. Then occurred a very evident change in his mood, and its expression in his art. His intense absorption in tragic experience is followed by a period of serenity and acquiescence. The atmosphere of all the plays of these last days is genial: the art is flexible and easy, the temper of the author is of one reconciled to the ways of God and man. Those authorities who think that the tragedies grew primarily out of the dramatist's personal experience assert that after the prolonged strain put upon imagination and feeling in the outpouring of his bitterness, Shakespeare suffered a break-down, followed by a readjustment of his attitude toward life, equivalent to a conversion.

Others are equally confident that the abrupt change in subject and spirit was due to a difference in the popular taste. With the enthronement of James, somber tragedies went out of favor, and in their place were substituted romances and tragic comedies. Beaumont and Fletcher grew in popularity as they lowered the prevailing tone of the stage. Shakespeare, say these scholars, met the dominant mood half-way. But 'he was too much interested in character portrayal, too truly an artist, too much enamored of lofty ethical ideals to prostitute his genius by adopting morally unwholesome plots. His lovers were romantic, not sentimental or pathological.'

The new fashions in play-writing, the natural reaction of Shakespeare's imagination after having been held ten years in the black air of tragedy, go far to explain this pronounced turn to romance. But in reading the plays of this period we must constantly bear in mind that we have to do with the most extraordinary poetic imagination humanity has yet produced. Shakespeare may have worked easily, even casually, but he worked powerfully and he worked truly. One may think romantically and yet think profoundly.

Surely serenity and reconciliation are the finest achievement of a long, experienced, and sane life. Acquiescence in the Scheme of Things, charity which suffereth long and is kind, trust in the goodness and wisdom of 'our veiled God,' these are the reward of a life greatly lived. In such a calm and luminous temper the meaning of things appears most clearly revealed.

Shakespeare is now in the fullness of his strength. Having learned his art, he uses it without strain and with joy; leisurely, almost as a plaything. He abates nothing in his recognition of evil, its weakness, its wickedness, and its disastrous effects. Only now it does not prevail. He has caught the deeper harmony, and emphasizes those forces of grace which are constantly bringing good out of evil, and causing the baser to minister to the higher. This more genial spirit appears first in *Pericles*. When we read these strong majestic sentences:

> Thou god of this great vast, rebuke these surges,
> Which wash both heaven and hell; and thou, that hast
> Upon the winds command, bind them in brass,
> Having call'd them from the deep!

we seem to have entered a brave new world in which man has dominion. We feel as Dante did when, issuing from the murk of the Inferno, he saw the tremulous sea and the dawn of Easter morning.

In *Antony and Cleopatra* and in *Coriolanus* Shakespeare traces wrath and lust through tragedy to reconciliation and to virtues which elicit admiration. Then follow three romances — *Cymbeline*, *The Winter's Tale*, and *The Tempest* — in which the calmness and the ripe wisdom of the master's spirit are revealed most completely.

Cymbeline was so much esteemed by Tennyson that his copy of the play together with a wreath from Virgil's tomb was buried with him. The plot is loosely joined and impossible, but the heroine, Imogen, is 'more completely drawn than any of his female characters' and possesses the highest charms of womanhood. She is 'a temple of virtue' against whom cruel slander, malignant intrigue, crafty villainy cannot avail. The atmosphere is not one of retribution but forgiveness.

> The fingers of the powers above do tune
> The harmony of this peace.

In giving Imogen the kiss of repentance and reconciliation Posthumus uttered the famous words;

> Hang there like fruit, my soul,
> Till the tree die!

The prevailing spirit of forgiveness is voiced in these words:

> Kneel not to me:
> The power that I have on you is to spare you,
> The malice towards you to forgive you: live,
> And deal with others better.

And Cymbeline speaks the final judgment:

> Pardon's the word to all.

In *The Winter's Tale* Leontes is mastered by a passion of jealousy as senseless and frenzied as that of Othello, but in these maturer years Shakespeare's imagination passes beyond the terror of ungoverned wrath and dwells upon the processes of reconciliation. Hermione evinces a fortitude which Desdemona did not possess.

> There's some ill planet reigns:
> I must be patient till the heavens look
> With an aspect more favorable. Good my lords,
> I am not prone to weeping, as our sex
> Commonly are, the want of which vain dew
> Perchance shall dry your pities; but I have
> That honourable grief lodg'd here which burns
> Worse than tears drown....

Desdemona was pathetic in helpless innocence; in Hermione Shakespeare is concerned with the conquering power of virtue. Leontes did not seek escape from his woe by suicide like Othello, but for sixteen years sought by prayer and good deeds to atone for his sin. Wisdom and purification came through suffering, and out of evil good issues. The central interest of the play is not in the tragic magnificence of unrestrained passion, but in the victorious power of shining and controlled virtue; not in the devastation of evil, as in *Othello*, but in the gentler forces which are superior to it.

Exceedingly valuable for our study is the last complete play Shakespeare wrote, *The Tempest*. It was acted at court in 1611 and again in 1613. There are strong reasons for thinking that in it the great dramatist was taking leave of the stage. He holds his wondrous Ariel in restraint for a few hours, promising him liberty when the task is done:

> ... I'll break my staff,
> Bury it certain fathoms in the earth,
> And, deeper than did ever plummet sound
> I'll drown my book.

And the epilogue strengthens the belief that more than the

closing of the play and the future of Prospero is hinted in
the words

> ... Now I want
> Spirits to enforce, art to enchant;
> And my ending is despair,
> Unless I be reliev'd by prayer.

In writing this romance Shakespeare enjoys the unac-
customed freedom of following his own inclinations. No
history or biography or tradition hampers him. The hero
Prospero is ruler of an enchanted island. All laws are
subject to his power. The author has perfect liberty, and
perfect liberty is a sure revealer of character. If the line of
thought we have followed throughout is true, if the most
comprehensive imagination our race has produced has during these years found its chief interest in understanding
and representing his world, then as he bids farewell to
the stage he would have urgent inducements to pass judgment upon the world he has experienced. Prospero on
his enchanted island is as free as God amid his worlds.
All spirits, men, and forces obey his will. In delineating
the manner in which an ideal man behaves toward his
fellows Shakespeare gives us a clear glimpse into his conception of the supreme qualities in human character.

The play opens on a tempest at sea caused by the magic
of Prospero. In a tossing vessel his enemies are in dire
distress. The scene then shifts to the enchanted island,
with Prospero telling his young daughter Miranda the
cause of their being in this isolated spot. When he was
Duke of Milan and absorbed in occult studies he had been
driven from his dukedom by his brother Antonio with the

connivance of Alonso, King of Naples. Their villainy had set him and his little daughter, then three years old, adrift on the sea in a rotten boat which had been carried by wind and current to this island. These events had taken place twelve years since. Amazed, Miranda exclaims:

> O the heavens!
> What foul play had we, that we came from thence?
> Or blessed was't we did?

Thus casually does this girl of fifteen touch the old problem of the relation of evil and freedom in the government of the world, and Shakespeare through Prospero answered it readily according to his well-considered philosophy of the 'soul of goodness in things evil':

> Both, both, my girl.
> By foul play, as thou say'st, were we heav'd thence,
> But blessedly holp hither.

By his profound knowledge the duke gained control of the island, enslaved Caliban, released the airy spirit Ariel, and mastered the elements by his magic art. Knowing his enemies to be on the sea in the same ship, Prospero has raised this fearful tempest, wrecked the vessel, and scattered the company about the island. Now that they are 'all knit up in their distractions' and completely in his grasp, how should he treat them? When one has all power how shall he deal with his enemies? Ariel, instructed by Prospero, answers in a stinging sermon on sin, one of the shortest and most powerful ever delivered, beginning, 'You are three men of sin.' He shows how powerless they are against the Higher Powers, who 'delaying, but not for-

getting' would requite their deeds, that 'a lingering perdi-
tion,' worse than any death, should attend them, and the
only guard against this just wrath

> ... is nothing but heart's sorrow
> And a clear life ensuing.

Alonso's conscience thunders at him through the roaring
winds and the deep-voiced billows, and to the extent of his
ability he makes amends. Antonio and Sebastian are
defiant, little realizing that at that moment they are at
the mercy of the man they have wronged. Ferdinand,
who had apparently been too roughly treated by Prospero,
learns that

> ... All thy vexations
> Were but my trials of thy love, and thou
> Hast strangely stood the test.

But Prospero was far from being merely a compound of
good nature. The recollection of the plot against him of
Caliban and his confederates awake in him strong anger.
Against his three chief enemies his wrath is hot, yet he
does not allow it to determine his actions.

> Though with their high wrongs I am struck to the quick,
> Yet with my nobler reason 'gainst my fury
> Do I take part. The rarer action is
> In virtue than in vengeance. They being penitent,
> The sole drift of my purpose doth extend
> Not a frown further.

Later he carries his magnanimity further in the excellent
advice,

> Let us not burden our remembrances with
> A heaviness that's gone.

Through the lips of Gonzalo Shakespeare interprets by the means of this plot his fundamental conviction that Providence works through evil for good issues:

> ... O, rejoice
> Beyond a common joy, and set it down
> With gold on lasting pillars: in one voyage
> Did Claribel her husband find at Tunis,
> And Ferdinand, her brother, found a wife
> Where he himself was lost, Prospero his dukedom
> In a poor isle, and all of us ourselves
> When no man was his own.

The opinion is widely held among scholars that in this last complete work from his pen, Shakespeare portrayed in Prospero the type of man he admired and strove to be. According to this the dramatist's ideal was a man of high intellectuality, yet capable of decisive action; one hurt by the foul ways of men, yet taking part with his nobler faculties against his baser impulses, who generously forgives a repentant enemy and does not burden his memory with an evil that is gone.

The poet's final judgment on life as he broke his magic staff was that working through the mystery and its evil was a kindly Providence which out of tempests of tribulations brought harmony, joy, and reconciliation.

He was helped to this attitude by his natural magnanimity of spirit. But his years of writing for the stage and his habit of thinking of life dramatically made him feel that life itself was but a play and the actors, moved by the Master of the Show, such stuff as dreams are made on. In these moments of detachment even the tragedies of life would not seem serious.

The Great Poets and the Meaning of Life

Like Dante, Shakespeare is reconciled to the universe because he discerns therein a Soul of Goodness which subdues at last the rages of the tempest to the harmonies of peace. The poet's closing years were serene because he trusted in the Lord of this Enchanted Island, set in this eternal sea, who restrained by his power the brutal Calibans, the murderers, and the foolish, and shaped the destinies of the good into paths of blessedness.

Summary

I come now to the hardest part of my task. Poets like Lucretius, Dante, Wordsworth wrote to instruct their readers, and each has a definite message which may be formulated. But Shakespeare is different. His aim was to please his audience and to understand his world. To use the drab word 'message' in connection with him is to drag glittering art from its seat of glory down to the uninspiring levels of homily and theology. Perhaps the least objectionable form of interrogation is to inquire what influences have entered into the spiritual life of England and the world which are more vital because they bear his charm and power. Upon what truths and faiths has he stamped his signet? To enumerate them is like counting the rays of light sparkling on a shimmering sea.

As I have pursued my studies in Shakespeare I have found that although his mind indeed flashes from many facets, it worked steadily upon certain fundamental assumptions, principles, admirations. These appeared at the beginning, they are found at the end of his work, more firmly believed, no less gloriously affirmed. Some of the most conspicuous and controlling of these I wish now to assemble.

No one has surpassed Shakespeare in making multitudes feel the radiancy of life. In his comedies it is the charm, the laughter, the wit and wisdom he discovers in the human scene which help to keep alive in the generations a zest for life. Because he found so much of mirth and meaning in men and women life is immensely more interesting to us.

In his early dramas on English history he is supremely concerned with what makes strong or weak the throne of kings. He stresses the moral framework of society and searches out the disasters which flow from crime and from feebleness. Evildoing disintegrates character, it leads to folly, it sends its destructions far and wide. He also discovered that where sin abounds forces of good are released to overcome the evil. There is some heroic quality in humanity which disaster makes more powerful and shining. The benefit of ill which he discovered in his youthful experience is confirmed in that couplet where discriminating wisdom is put in perfect form:

> There is some soul of goodness in things evil
> Would men observingly distil it out.

He admired and makes us admire, courage, honor, and above all magnanimity.

When Shakespeare, during the period of the tragedies, passed through the world's inferno, he journeyed as a poet eager to understand these damaged souls, not as a judge eager to condemn them. It is in the tragedies that he has his deepest vision into the meaning of life. In that high mood out of which these mighty dramas came, what did he see which appeared to him of sovereign significance?

Profound as was his penetration during those years, he beheld nothing which changed his conviction that man acts in freedom in a moral universe which is not slack or indifferent. What he asserted of moral law in his historical plays, he now asserts more startlingly in the tragedies. He assumes that the dominant cause of tragedy is the fact that man is a moral being, living under the laws of righteousness. Therefore there are sufferings in human lives which would be impossible if we were under the law of the jungle. The chief cause of horror is man's clash with the moral law — the law within and the law without. The undoing of Richard III was his attempt to live un-scrupulously in a world built on a different plan, which resulted in the protest of his own conscience, the hostility of an outraged kingdom and of the forces of the spiritual world, which arrayed themselves with Richmond. This teaching is put even more powerfully in *Macbeth*. Iago also is both hardened and blinded in his evil by the moral process within; energies working in the world about him light up his fiendish malignity and defeat his purposes. No other poet has described the rebite of sin with such frequency and magnificence of power.

Dante conceived of a moral system so perfectly bal-anced that every infringement demanded an equal re-quital. Sin makes a void which the sinner must fill with just penalties. The more philosophically minded among us hold an abstract conception of an august, inviolable moral order. But a dramatist's interest is in a concrete fact, not in abstract ideas, therefore he emphasizes not a moral order, but a moral process. He thought more in the Scriptural form of statement: Whatsoever a man soweth, that shall he also reap. It was the strong links binding retribution to sin that engaged his attention. This nemesis he studied with passion and presents in many forms.

No poet or prophet has imprinted this truth of the inevitable connection binding sin and punishment more indelibly upon the minds of men.

Shakespeare strengthens our faith in the providential ordering of events, and as subtlely as the most skilled metaphysician, and more forcibly than any other poet, draws the line between Divine sovereignty and human responsibility;

> There's a divinity that shapes our ends
> Rough-hew them how we will.

'Men at some time are masters of their fate.' 'Our thoughts are ours, their ends none of our own.'

It may possibly be objected that a dramatist must bind events together to obtain the desired result, and that his plan becomes the providence of his play. But our contention is that Shakespeare was much more than a playwright constructing a successful plot. He was one of the supreme poets of the world. He was pre-eminently fascinated with man and his experiences. He followed the subtle development of character and destiny with the same precision with which a surgeon's knife follows a nerve, or a diagnostician seeks the cause of symptoms. He recognized so often the presence of a Power, not ourselves, that is working for righteousness, and proclaimed it with such accents of sincerity that, I think, we may affirm confidently that he has added vitality to our faith in a Divinity that shapes our ends, and confirms our belief that through our moral intuitions we glimpse Reality, even if only as in a mirror, darkly.

According to Aristotle, the function of tragedy is to represent human nobility as well as human villainy. Where evil is given its largest freedom and amplest triumph it serves to disclose a spiritual grandeur in the soul of man which is superior to the assaults of evil and the wreckage of fortunes. No poet has equaled Shakespeare in ability to exhibit the towering splendor of this quality in men. He touches goodness with his enchantment and it assumes celestial glory.

His fascination with this theme appeared first in the *Rape of Lucrece*, published when he was thirty. In the heroine he delineated a spiritual chastity which could not be defiled and of which tribulation simply unveiled the luster. This exaltation of womanly purity may have been a convention of the poetry of the day which he adopted, but this emphasis on transcendent virtue appearing in the earlier poem continues, and strengthens through the years. In the period of the comedies his youthful imagination was attracted to woman's wit, beauty, and innocence. In the period of the tragedies he confronted moral evil in its most terrific and abhorrent forms. But in this murk and welter he discovered virtues which the assault of fiendish forces revealed and disciplined, but could not conquer. In his heroes and heroines he affirmed again and again that there is something in the human spirit that pays no homage either to chance or sin. This shining spiritual integrity, these virtues which plead like angels, make one feel the greatness of humanity, the changeless beauty of courage and high honor.

To set forth heroic qualities in men and incorruptible chastity and fidelity in women is not uncommon in literature, but no writer has equaled Shakespeare in making virtue glow with enchantment, or flash forth in so many forms its power to conquer evil.

His sense of the greatness of the human spirit when tried in the extreme found voice in Hamlet's spontaneous tribute to humanity's high and varied qualities. Hamlet could utter them because they were familiar thoughts of the poet:

> What a piece of work is a man! How noble in reason! How infinite in faculty! In form and moving how express and admirable! In action how like an angel! In apprehension how like a god! The beauty of the world! The paragon of animals!'

Into the final period of the romances he carries the same principles, admirations, assumptions which have dominated his work from the beginning; evil is still malignant and foolish, and retribution is certain; wisdom is learned through suffering, and, after evil has done its worst, there remains something in the human soul which is beyond its power and is a source of peace and victory. In the tragedies the dramatist paused before the horror of evil; in his final writings he goes beyond and acclaims the nobility of forgiveness and the possibility of reconciliation. And almost his last words call attention to the unsubstantial pageantry of the world and the folly of taking it too seriously.

Throughout his plays Shakespeare's treatment of evil has this marked peculiarity. He has 'no innocent adulteries, no interesting incests, no virtuous vice; he never renders that amiable which religion and reason alike teach us to detest, or clothes impurity with the garb of virtue.' He follows the great tradition of poets and prophets in portraying the excess of egoism as the essence of sin. 'I follow but myself,' declares Iago. He puts many evil men and women on the stage and allows them to prosper in their wrongdoing, but such is his art that one does not admire his villains, even in their success.

No poet in the long history of genius has ever expressed so much wisdom in an ultimate form. To say wise words is difficult, but to say them in a manner that cannot be improved is a supreme test of intellectual ascendancy. De Maupassant has written, 'Whatever may be the thing one wishes to say there is only one phrase to express it, only one verb to animate it, only one adjective to qualify it.' This is forcibly stated, yet I should like to add 'only one cadence to propel it.' Every idea carries with it its appropriate emotion. To formulate a thought without the emotional rhythm proper to it is to deprive it of much of its glory and power. Sentences which live forever are as memorable for their form as for their substance. Such sentences come from the depths of a rich and experienced personality. Outside the authorized version of the Scriptures, no book contains so much truth shaped with perfect grace as Shakespeare's works.

Mr. Santayana says that 'Shakespeare was notable among the greater poets as being without a philosophy and without a religion; he failed to give life a dramatic unity.' Continuing he says: 'A fine sense of the dignity and pathos of life cannot be attained unless we conceive somehow its outcome and its relations; without it the imagination cannot fulfil its function or achieve its supreme success.' There is truth in this, as both Dante and Milton bear witness. But is Mr. Santayana quite true to the facts? Shakespeare indeed does not dogmatize concerning the outcome of experience and life as Lucretius does, as Dante does. But he has penetrating and comprehensive insights into the nature of things which have deeply stirred men's hearts. He may not have had any interest in uniting these into a philosophy, yet in their isolation they have ministered to heroic faith. He could not affirm immortality with the confidence of Dante, who said, 'Of all stupidities that is the most foolish, the basest, and the most pernicious, which believes that after this life there is no other.' Again: ' ... and so I believe, so aver, and so am certain of the passage after this life to another better life.' But Shakespeare has uttered great words which strengthen a believer's faith in something beyond death. In the sonnets he finds consolation in the truth that the soul grows strong even in the body's loss:

> So shalt thou feed on death, that feeds on men,
> And Death once dead, there's no more dying then.

The world's faith has laid hold of the instinctive cry of Horatio as a fine expression of a reasonable hope:

> Good night, sweet prince,
> And flights of angels sing thee to thy rest!

In another powerful way Shakespeare helps us conceive the outcome of life. From Brutus to Prospero and Queen Katherine he ceaselessly reiterates the thought that there is something in the soul that does not yield to disaster but is ennobled by it. Neither does Shakespeare fail to set life in its larger 'relations.' In the tragedies he thunders unequivocally of man's relationship to the law within and the law without. Just as unequivocally he teaches in all his later plays one's true attitude toward his fellows, an attitude of forbearance, mercy, and magnanimity. His pages contain no such symbol of the supreme Determiner of Destiny as fill the closing pages of the *Divine Comedy* with celestial light, but he has, in Portia's immortal plea, made men feel, as no other poet has, the divinity of mercy. Neither could he have brought himself to have uttered with sincerity those terrible words of Thomas Hardy, 'The President of the immortals has ended his sport with Tess.'

In contrast his words in *Titus Andronicus* have exerted a very different influence:

> Wilt thou draw near the nature of the gods?
> Draw near them, then, in being merciful;
> Sweet mercy is nobility's true badge.

Doubtless his dramas lack a unified philosophy, but no poet has done more to strengthen confidence in the providential ordering of events or proclaimed more powerfully the worth and the glory of justice, mercy, and that charity which understanding all forgives all. He presents the ultimate truths to our emotions and imaginations, not to our speculative reason. Shakespeare had in a superlative degree what the Hebrews called the 'understanding heart.' Out of this priceless possession issued his pity, his tolerance, his admirations, his moral judgments, and his serenity.

They were in himself and he impressed them on the world. But Shakespeare's chief contribution to the life of the spirit was himself. Few would dissent from the assertion that one of the world's most grievous needs is imagination, the ability to put one's self in the other man's place and look at questions from his point of view. Out of the stupid blindness of minds lacking in imagination have grown most of the persecution, hatreds, wars which have cursed humanity. Shakespeare is pre-eminent among poets; yes, and among prophets and moralists, for his sympathetic imagination. With it he entered into the secrets of all sorts and conditions of men. Seeing intensely and comprehensively, he understood, he had compassion, he was tolerant, he was merciful, he was serene. A penetrating and catholic imagination made him a great poet; it also made him a great man. To say of one that he has caught the spirit of Shakespeare is to say that he surpasses his fellows in catholicity and balance of mind. He will be a man faithful in friendship, calm in adversity, exquisitely sensitive to the beautiful in nature and character, and possessing that quality of mirth which keeps the moral temper sweet and sound.

THE SUPREME EPIC:
Religion as Poetry

NATURALLY the study of the great poets would now take us to the consideration of Milton and *Paradise Lost* — the noblest epic creation in the English speech — then to Goethe and the spiritual adventures of Faust. But our purpose is to substitute for these a discussion of a book which is a world epic in a sense true of no other writings bound between two covers.

To classify it as an epic is venturesome and perhaps unwarranted, yet it has the epic spirit, the epic material, the epic purpose, the epic story, and the epic style. It is a world epic in the sense that it is the fruitage of many and great empires, for the Babylonian, the Hebrew, the Greek, the Roman, the English civilizations, have all contributed to its substance and molded its form. Drawing from many nations, it has been world-wide in its influence.

I refer to the authorized version of the English Bible. That its tale of spiritual adventure is epic in range and in interest; that its style is in the grand manner, there can be no question. It is debatable whether we are justified in extending the word 'epic' to cover its peculiar characteristics.

THE SUPREME EPIC: *Religion as Poetry*

What is an Epic?

It is well known that we inherit our literary classifications from the Greeks. When Aristotle in the *Poetics* described the nature of the epic he had for his models the *Iliad* and the *Odyssey*, and his authority has been great. Since his day many heroic poems have claimed consideration as epics, and the term has been stretched to include the *Niebelungenlied*, the *Mahabharata*, the *Æneid*, *Paradise Lost*, and the *Song of Roland*. Amid these diversities of form and substance, there are certain characteristics which we expect to find in a genuine epic. We look for a story, nobly told, recounting the adventures of a hero and his victorious struggle with foes without and foes within; it moves to a stately measure and is poetic in spirit and in form; it appeals to the common hopes, fears, and beliefs of men; it is representative of the legends of the people from whom it sprang and symbolizes some vital aspect of human destiny; its author is the spirit of a people, speaking through one transcendent poet, or through many minstrels. The epics of art are unified and colored by the genius of the author; the epics of growth are the accretions of the thoughts of many minds and many generations.

Let us now turn our attention to the story of spiritual adventure recorded in the Old and New Testaments, and observe to what extent it corresponds to the epic requirements.

First, we find it to be a tale of deep human interest, most engagingly narrated. In the process of its development it unifies a notable variety of literature into a whole and discloses a continuous and progressive plot. Tradition, poetry, history, allegory, vision have been organized; the books have become a Book, because they are the documents of an unfolding adventure.

It opens with a majestic Hymn of Creation, whose first line as definitely strikes the keynote of all that follows as do the epics of ancient tradition. We remember Virgil's 'Arms and the man I sing,' Homer's 'Achilles wrath,' Milton's 'Of man's first disobedience and the fruit Of that forbidden tree,' as we catch the opening note whose solemn music and grandeur of significance sets high the theme of all that follows: 'In the beginning God created the heaven and the earth'; then follows the mythology of the Hebrew people as related to this theme, changing into three cycles of legends concerning the traditional ancestors of the people; the tribes have dramatic experiences, they become slaves, nomadic wanderers under a leader of heroic breed, they conquer a country, they establish a kingdom and a religion. Then appear a succession of extraordinary men who are prophets and statesmen, endowed richly with the gift of poetic utterance, who wrote down what the Eternal said to them. Soon the kingdom is divided, the capital destroyed, and by the waters of Babylon the people weep bitter tears. They returned to a ruined country, facing poverty, hardship, disillusionment, which were lightened by a vast and glorious hope of a Conqueror who would come to make this feeble folk the ruler and guide of the nations. Accompanying this stirring narrative are collections of marvelous lyrics through which they poured out their hearts to the Almighty, the incomprehensible, the merciful God who held them as a peculiar possession. Here are their wise proverbs, their marriage songs, their code of laws, turned by the poetic mind of the race into resonant oratory, which at times lifts itself to great poetry. The Old Testament ends in a night of despair lighted with the burning hope of the Deliverer.

It is a very human story, the struggle is epic in intensity and significance, the purpose epic in grandeur; but epics do not end in prostration and defeat. The theme is continued in the New Testament. The Expected One comes, attended by celestial portents at his birth, authenticated by power of miracles. But his guise was not what the eager nation expected; they looked for a Lion of the Tribe of Judah and beheld a lamb as it had been slain. To an ever-enlarging group he was the Redeemer foretold by the prophets. He is crucified, yet rises again, the number of believers increases, they speak of him as the Logos, the Son of God, the Power by whom all things were created. Then we are told of the deadly conflict of the Church with the Roman Empire; the story closing with a sublime prophetic vision of the triumph of the Son of God and the complete subjugation of Satan and his hosts, with the Conqueror seated at the right hand of the Almighty. It is a unified spiritual experience, epic in majesty, intensity, and meaning.

Again, this romance of spiritual adventure is not lacking in a Hero. But who is the Hero? Certainly it is not Adam, who occupies a central place for a few verses only. Neither is it Humanity, or even Israel, for the Hebrew never looked upon mankind as in any sense heroic, and Israel he considered a servant, a thing to be redeemed, not the originator of conquering power. The nearest approach to a Hero who unifies the thought and passion of the Old Testament is the expected Messiah. And this part of the story closes with the hero yet to come. Ending with a disillusioned and defeated people who only dream of future deliverance, the Old Testament by itself is but a truncated epic. The narrative must continue into the New Testament, the Hero must come, the victory must at least be assured, if the Scriptures are to take on the character of an epic. There will be no dissent regarding the Hero here presented. The growing faith in the disturbing figure of Jesus is clearly traced. At first a mighty prophet, then the Messiah, then the redeemer of the world through his sufferings, then his humanity seems lost in the splendor of God which shone through him, then in the thought of believers he takes on cosmic significance. Paul declared that this divine redemptive power which appeared in Jesus was engaged in its saving work during the Old Testament dispensation — 'The fathers drank of the spiritual Rock that followed them, and the Rock was Christ.' And in the first chapter of Colossians there are words, probably quoted from a hymn of the ancient church, which affirm that in him were all things created and that in him all things consist. In the Gospel of John this same creative, redeeming spirit is called the Logos, the Word. It formed the glory that was in Jesus. In him it was the Eternal Light, coming into the world.

It is not germane to the present discussion to pass upon

the truth of these tremendous affirmations, but in this I think there will be general agreement: if one takes up the English Bible, searching for the Hero whose victorious struggles, whose will and purpose and spirit bind all the contents into a unity, that Hero is the Logos, the Word, that quality in the Eternal which enters into time and space, creates man, and works through him to accomplish a divine purpose. Or to change from theological language to epic phraseology, the Hero is the God-Man, the ever-living Son, who like the gods of the *Iliad* appears in many forms. The men whose spiritual imagination brought all these various books into a single book were profoundly certain that from the beginning there had been an unfolding purpose working in history, through individuals, through Israel, through ancient empires, through Jesus of Nazareth, for the redemption of the world. This Eternal Energy they called by different names — the Logos, the Living Christ, the Son of God, but he worked in the Old Testament and the New, weaving them into an epic unity. He is working in the world today, the aeonian struggle is still going on, and not until the end of time will the perfect epic be completed.

An epic cannot be a 'great story, greatly told' unless the author's purpose has vital significance for human destiny. In the *Iliad* Homer criticizes life by lifting over the common ways of men figures of heroic courage; Virgil's design is to hold the Romans to a high ideal of their divine mission to the world; Milton would justify the ways of God to men.

That the purpose of the book which came out of Palestine is epic in range and grandeur there can be no debate. It would reveal how the seed of the woman shall bruise the serpent's head, how man may become more than conqueror, and attain the felicity of perfect freedom and peace. It meets completely the definition which Mr. Routh, in his volume entitled *God, Man and Epic Poetry*, lays down: 'An epic shows how the burden of fear falls off and the spirit springs up to its superhuman stature.' It keeps its consistency to type by showing victory over some form of human weakness. Victory over evil through which man comes to 'superhuman stature' is the central theme of the Scriptures.

An epic must come out of and appeal to the elemental passions and beliefs of men. This is eminently true of the book we consider the supreme epic.

> Out from the heart of nature rolled
> The burdens of the Bible old;
> The litanies of nations came,
> Like the volcano's tongue of flame,
> Up from the burning core below —
> The canticles of love and woe.

And these burdens are not the burdens of Israel only, they mirror the general experiences of man; therefore they are readily translated into every tongue. Here also the epic spirit through this long adventure breathes a passion which kindles fidelity, sympathy, and dauntless courage.

An epic must have a sustained nobility of style. In this respect the English Bible is not found wanting. Many writers have paid a just tribute to the long roll of the heroic hexameter, but the authorized version of the

Scriptures has a measure by no means less stately and majestic. It is a style eminently becoming a world epic because it was not formed by the genius of any particular people. The chief languages of the world brought their glory and honor into it. It is founded on Hebrew thought and passion, hence its sublimity, simplicity, and throb of strong emotion. Then the Hebrew Testament was translated into Greek and became the Septuagint, and the New Testament was written by men who were influenced in idiom and philosophy by the habits of the Greek mind. Then the book passed into a world dominated by the majestic language of Rome, and the Vulgate conveyed Hebrew thought and feeling in stately and resonant Latin. The grandeur that was Rome penetrated and transformed the English speech and the book which was to become its noblest monument. For over a thousand years the Psalms were sung and the services said in the sonorous Latin tongue. Every one of the King James translators had from his youth formed his taste on its music. Then came William Tyndale, a genius in translation, who put the New Testament and part of the Old into the vital English of the early sixteenth century. Tyndale, deadly in earnest to release the stupendous truths of the Scriptures in words the plow boy could understand, set the standard of terseness, dignity, and force for all the versions which have followed. After him for some eighty-five years English scholars were busy making the Scriptures effective to the nation. And the result was the King James Version, published in 1611. It is a monument to the piety, the good taste, and the ability of English scholarship. Every sentence, every word, every cadence was tested most searchingly. The resulting style is not English. It is unlike anything in our literature, except the books which sprang from it. It is not Hebrew, nor Greek, nor Latin in the ring of its words or the sweep of its sentences. It is neither Oriental nor Occidental. It is the thought and passion of the East uttered in the most virile speech of the West, modified by the precision of the Greek, the deep, long music of the Latin, with now and then a touch of the German, the French, and the Italian.

> But here is the finger of God, a flash of the will that can,
> Existent behind all laws, that made them and, lo, they are!
> And I know not if, save in this, such gift be allowed to man,
> That out of three sounds he frame, not a fourth sound, but a star.

The resultant from the mingling in this book of the languages and the thoughts of great civilizations is a wonder of style which is not Hebrew, nor Greek, nor Latin, nor English, but a new splendor shining upon the world.

Let us give more detailed attention to the unique style of this world epic. In a book written by Hebrews of widely different temperaments and conditions the idiosyncrasies of the writers have been obscured because neither Greek, Roman, nor English translators tried to preserve them. This fusion of the many into the one has resulted in a characteristic Biblical diction which is easily recognized. Language has two functions — to express thought and to convey emotion. The best words are those which frame intellectual conceptions with precision, and communicate most effectually the feelings appropriate to the thought.

The Supreme Epic: *Religion as Poetry*

The words must be so arranged that their overtones stir the emotions.

The translators of the English Bible who stand in the recognized succession have been for the most part men who were much more than accurate linguists; they were mindful of the fact that rhythm is fundamental to all the arts; they were concerned with the thought, but also they took infinite pains to release the beauty and the passion of the thought. The Bishops' Bible in Isaiah 53:3 reads, 'He is such a man as hath good experience of sorrows and infirmities.' This states a fact in an ineffectual way. The sentence is dead. But one scholar had enough poetry in his soul to appreciate the pathos of the thought and wrote, 'He was a man of sorrows and acquainted with grief.' This is memorable speech, fit for oratorios, and sings its way into the heart. Pervading the Sermon on the Mount there is the 'penetrative music which informs great prose.' Take the words found in Matthew 6:25 as translated in a modern version.

> Therefore I tell you, do not trouble about what you are to eat or drink in life, nor what you are to put on your body; surely life means more than food; surely the body means more than clothes!... Which of you can add an ell to his height by troubling about it? And why should you trouble over clothing? Look how the lilies of the field grow.

The rich comfort of the thought is held back by such prosaic sentences. The restful harmonies of the message are broken by the unloveliness of the lines.

Now let the reader permit the words as translated in the authorized version to run through his mind; they are as melodious and restful as a mountain brook. The form is as gracious as the thought, and conveys the full meaning of the truth.

We know that our sensibilities are stirred in proportion to the vividness of the picture in the mind. 'Consider the lilies' introduces a clear image; holding this in our thought we can turn to contemplate how they grow. But to be challenged with 'Look how!' leaves our mind groping.

If one is not quite certain what Matthew Arnold meant by the 'grand manner' of the immortal writers, let him sense the difference between 'Consider the lilies of the field how they grow,' and 'Look how the lilies of the field grow.'

For a line memorable through its harmony of truth and form, recall the opening sentences of the Nineteenth Psalm: 'The heavens declare the glory of God, and the firmament showeth his handiwork.' This is sublime, but it is not the sublimity of Burke, or Milton, or Webster. That lofty music is not of the West. It has the austere simplicity of thought and mood of the Hebrew put into English rhythm. It is a great sentence because it expresses as precisely as language is able the thoughts and the emotions of a reverent and profound mind mastered by the glory of the heavens.

Mr. Kipling in a magazine article written shortly before his death imagined that he detected Shakespeare's delicate touch in the opening and closing verses of the sixtieth chapter of Isaiah, so glowingly do the words communicate the lofty passion. The peculiar note of the trumpet is *ai, ai*. Note the trumpet ring in 'Arise, shine; for thy light is come.'

The Supreme Epic: *Religion as Poetry*

The poet who wrote: 'Where wast thou when I laid the foundations of the earth?... When the morning stars sang together, and all the sons of God shouted for joy?' had an imagination capable of a great epic or a hallelujah chorus. The reader more than receives an idea; he feels immeasurable time, the solemn glory of space, and a joy that must be shouted. He sees a brave new world.

One might continue almost indefinitely quoting sentences enchanting because they kindle the imagination, or so cadenced that the accent brings out perfectly the feeling the thought requires. Only a scholar with active fountains of poetry in his soul should attempt to translate the world's supreme epic.

I think I have presented sufficient evidence to carry the reader's assent to the proposition that the authorized version of the Scriptures is a true and powerful epic in the following particulars: it has its unity in a story that is epical in sweep and meaning; it has a Hero more completely human, more indubitably divine than the heaven-descended heroes of other epics; through the volume runs the epic purpose to declare to humanity its nature, destiny, and victory; it has a loftier epic mood, and epic material more universal, than any other song of the nations; and all is clothed in language of unique power which expresses common things simply and great things gloriously.

What the Bible lacks of being patently the world's supreme epic is Form. We expect an epic to be a long poem. If the substance of the Bible, instead of being shaped by redactors and selected by ecclesiastical committees, had been sung in heroic verse by some poet of commanding

227

genius, like Isaiah, it would then conform quite completely to the definitions imposed by literary orthodoxy.

But if the Bible is not poetical in form, it is poetical in substance. Most of its material has been shaped by a poetry-loving people; its great prophets are poets of unquestionable rank; its psalms, after these many centuries, are still the most adequate outpouring of our religious feelings; Job is reckoned as one of the world's masterpieces, Proverbs and Ecclesiastes are conspicuously poetical both in thought and style and Deuteronomy sounds an organ note not unlike that of Milton.

Passing to the New Testament, we find that Jesus had the feelings and the intuitive mind of a poet; in his words are poetic fire and poetic melody. Paul's imperishable chapters, lifting high our conceptions of love, of humanity clothed with immortality, of the joy, peace, and power of them that are in Christ Jesus, are of the loftiest poetic strain and have sung themselves into the hearts of multitudes. Milton called Revelation 'the majestic image of a high and stately tragedy, shutting up and intermingling her solemn scenes and acts with a seven fold chorus of hallelujahs and harping symphonies.'

The Scriptures are poetically conceived as a whole; they are saturated with poetry and they affect the reader in the fashion of great poetry. But they are not in the form of epic verse. Can the conception of an epic be enlarged to embrace works which are not in numbers? The Oxford Dictionary thinks this is legitimate. It reads: 'The typical epics, the Homeric poems, the Nibelungenlied &c. have often been regarded as embodying a nation's conception of its own past history, or of events in that history which it finds most worthy of remembrance. Hence by some writers the phrase national epic has been applied to any imaginative work (whatever its form) which is considered to fulfil this function.' That is, this latest dictionary grants that the conception of an epic is capable of development; it recognizes that a work which records in high seriousness a nation's ideal and experience, poetically conceived, may be called an epic 'whatever its form.' The fathers did not permanently fix the molds of art or of thought. 'They didn't know everything down in Judee,' nor in Athens.

The Old Testament is a national epic in the sense that it represents Israel's conception of its past history and the events 'most worthy of remembrance.' The New Testament continues and interprets the Old by setting down what the Church thought 'most worthy of remembrance' in its past history. The two, brought together in a continuous story, are found to express what many peoples 'find most worthy of remembrance' and constitute an epic which is more than national. Representing, as it does, the thought of the East and the language of the West, the English Bible is a world epic in a sense which is true of no other monument of human experience.

In other respects this epic differs from the common definition. Notice that, unlike the Greek and Latin epics, it does not exalt man. It does not sing of arms and the man. Its victories are not on the field of battle, but are inner conquests for the control of the springs of action. Its commanding virtue is obedience, not fortitude. Man is a servant, a follower, a co-laborer, not a superb hero, magnificently asserting his will, and, by his resourcefulness and power, establishing his supremacy. Not the amazing glories of man, but the glory of God is central in the Scriptures. 'Man is but dust,' is the confession murmured on every page. 'Thine is the kingdom and the power and the glory.'

To put in a few words my contention: We have in our most cherished literary treasure the story of a spiritual adventure which is epical in the profoundest and loftiest sense of the word. The Hero of the New Testament is the divine man Jesus Christ. The thought pervading the book is that the spiritual life that shone in splendor in this man was not of time, but had been working from the beginning until that day. This timeless spirit, manifest in Jesus, is called by various names, the Logos, the God-Man, the Living Christ, the Humanity in God. It is represented as engaged in an age-long battle with evil. This struggle has cosmic significance; it is real and desperate. Traveling in the greatness of his strength down through the ages and through nations, this God-Man, this Eternal Word, is meeting, with battle agony and yet victoriously, the sins and the evil of the world. Ultimately He will conquer completely. Death and hell shall be put under his feet, and He shall deliver up the kingdom to his Father that God may be all in all.

The theme is epical in magnificence. Epic is its material, epic its purpose, and epic the glory of its language. It exceeds the accepted definitions to this extent that it introduces much in prose form, and it emphasizes, not the heroic virtues of man, but the grace of God. And its author, far from being a single poet, or group of gifted men, is a succession of bold, poetic, and saintly minds extending through many generations. It is more than a national, it is a human epic.

But why spend so much space and heat over the mere matter of enlarging the meaning of a word? The book is in a class by itself; why labor to bring it under any accepted literary classification? My purpose in this discussion has been to focus the reader's attention on the very intimate relations existing between religion and poetry, to show how largely our noblest spiritual conceptions partake of the nature of great poetry. Many of the darkest tragedies of history would never have occurred had not learned men mistaken the outpourings of high emotions and the utterance of towering aspirations as matter-of-fact statements, and interpreted them as prosaically as they would a lawbook. It is the poetry of faith and hope and love which make the Scriptures an ever-living thing. When Religion ceases to sing and seeks the poor defense of dogma, she is dying. If the Church had sung the lofty truths contained in the Nicene Creed, as Thomas Arnold suggested, and had recognized how impotent metaphysics is to give form and effect to the verities of the faith, much agony would have been spared. How futilely our keen and undaunted theologians have tried to compass the vast mysteries of life in the logic of their little systems!

Our speech was born of the imagination; our words are faded pictures, ancient metaphors. Our language at best is symbolic of actuality, not a transcription of it. The highest truths of religion are beyond the power of our minds to define, God, his nature and purpose; immortality, its character and glory, these exceed the scope of our reasoning and our conceptual ability. Eye hath not seen, nor ear heard, nor the heart of man conceived them as they are. Therefore to convey our thought of the invisible we use symbols, and symbols are only suggestions, pictures to hold the imagination, something for thought to stand on.

As we cannot compass in our conceptions the Infinite and Eternal, the religious mind has searched through nature for its most exalted and meaningful symbol. With astonishing unanimity it has selected Light. For light is that point in the material world where matter becomes so attenuated that it seems to merge into the spiritual. But religious faith desires something more personal as the interpreter of the Supreme. It believes that in man there is a forth-shining of God more splendid than the radiance of the sun's disc, and Christendom has turned to the spirit of Jesus as the largest and clearest lens interpreting the encompassing mystery.

To enforce her truths the Church has recourse to the imagination. When she wishes to assert that Jesus exerts an influence whose quality and authority is like that of God, she abandons prose as incompetent, and appealing to the imagination, confesses, poetically and vividly, that 'He sitteth at the right hand of God, the Father Almighty.' This is not the description of a fact; it is faith speaking in the most effective manner. What fierce debates, what martyr fires, what schisms in the body of Christ would have been avoided if ecclesiastical dignitaries had sensed the impossibility of constraining in their metaphysics and dialectics the realities of the kingdom of the spirit! Our fathers could not define the substance of a blade of grass. Why were they so confident that they could draw the line between the substance of the divine and human? Religion is never so secure or so irresistible as when she boldly uses the methods and spirit of poetry, its colorful words, its types, its imagery. Her days are great when she lays hold of the imagination. It is the prose in the theological and hierarchical soul that has brought sorrow and weakness to the Church.

How completely the Bible uses the methods of poetry to set forth its tremendous facts and teachings! It opens with a great poem of measured beauty; a story reveals the nature of sin. Its early history is composed largely of the traditions of the common people, shaped and colored by the imagination; the most illustrious of the prophets were poets, for them the mountains broke forth into singing, and the trees clapped their hands; the psalmists sang the needs of men in patterned speech. The spiritual leaders of the people for the most part used language, not with meticulous precision, but artistically, rapturously. They spoke in hyperbole with exaggerated emphasis that they might arouse stolid, indifferent minds. Our Lord had the intuitive mind of a poet and employed a poet's method; his words had rare grace as well as power; he used them startlingly to produce lasting effects. He embodied truth in a tale that it might enter in at lowly doors, his parables were finished pictures, his prophecies of judgment rolled forth like solemn music. He did not speak as the scribes with calculated precision, but poetically in strong words glowing with emotion.

To Paul the Christian was a warrior, armed for battle, contending with the principalities and powers of darkness. John visualized the final blessedness in the figure of a great multitude, clothed in white, standing with waving palms before a great white throne, and reprobation as a lake of fire.

The glory of poetry shines everywhere in the Scriptures; its history and its truths are poetically conceived, and the Way of Life from the beginning to the end forms for the imagination an unforgettable picture.

To use a phrase of Horace Bushnell's, the Gospel is 'a gift to the imagination.' The Church has never completely subordinated the poetical qualities of its faith to its arid metaphysics. It has lived because it is drenched with poetry. The mass is a drama, the Lord's Supper a sacrament. She teaches through altars, candles, pictures, hymns, and eloquent speech. Down the centuries she has reached the heart through the imagination.

To call the Bible a supreme epic and to relate it so closely to poetry does not diminish its authority; it enhances it. It changes emphasis from fact to idea. If the stronghold of religion is in its historical facts and in the logic of its reasonings, it is continually open to the assaults of the critic. But its commanding ideas, known to be truth through the fiery experience of many generations, are immortal and speak with divine power to the hearts of men.

It was Aristotle's judgment that poetry possesses a greater truth and a higher seriousness than history. It

234

has values of real worth which a record of facts does not have. This is an important consideration, too often forgotten in an age of research and criticism, an age hot on the trail of facts. Facts are important, but poetry and religion deal with them in such a manner as to give them greater veracity and graver import. A chronicle narrates events, a history puts events into some kind of relationship to other events, making either a picture or a philosophy; the poet takes the supposed events and presents their meaning to human life, the nourishment they give to our hope, our comfort, our faith. The fact, under the wizardry of the imagination, becomes a truth, glorified, personal, clothed with power. Poetry has a higher truth than history precisely as a painting contains something of value not to be seen in a photograph. The tragedy of *Hamlet* voices truths not to be found in the biography of the Prince of Denmark. Poetry is the language of lofty emotion, it is speech at its utmost of energy and beauty. Therefore it appeals to the imagination, the thought, the heart of man with a weight which history, minus the poetic quality, cannot possess.

Religion treats facts and ideas in the same way. To her they are revelations of the spiritual order which surrounds the world of the senses. She uses them for the enrichment of life, her methods are the methods of poetry, her language avoids the precision of the scientist; it is symbolical, artistic, designed to quicken thought and emotion.

Alike as religion and poetry are in their material and machinery, they have decided differences. A man of strong religious nature feels that his faith and its objects have a solid worth which does not pertain to poetry. Both give liberty, peace, and elevation of being. But the peace of poetry issues from a sense of harmony; the peace of religion results from a sense of security, of resting upon a Rock, of being guided by a Superior Wisdom.

Poetry is most fruitful to us in our hours of adequacy, when at least we are not submerged by the waves and billows of trouble. Its usefulness is more limited to our moods and condition. It is in weakness that the strength of religion is made perfect; with poetry it is not so.

Again religion has more of ethical insistence. To her truth becomes a law, and vision does not end in ecstasy, but in character and conduct. There is substantial truth in Santayana's affirmation that when religion does not interfere with our way of living, it is poetry; when poetry influences character and conduct it becomes our religion.

Most poetry is an idealization of things seen and felt, and its power lies in the charm of the idealization; in religion the final emphasis is on the reality of the stuff of which the ideal is formed. Reality has a prominence in religion which it does not have in poetry. Religion is willing to acknowledge that her conceptions of God are utterly inadequate, they are but broken lights, but they are broken lights of Thee, the supreme Reality. She acknowledges that her language is symbolic, but it is symbolic of that which was, and is, and is to be.

Religion rests more heavily on the facts of history, colored although they may be through long tradition and popular imagination. Holding tenaciously the conviction that a divine purpose is working progressively through the ages, she is seriously concerned with the truths established by human experience.

Yet great verse and high religion are of closest kin. Mr. Santayana, in his discussion of poetry and religion, writes these illuminating words:

> Poetry is metrical and euphuistic discourse expressing thought which is both sensuous and ideal. Such is poetry as a literary form; but if we drop the limitation as to verbal expression, and think of poetry as that subtle fire and inward light which seems to shine through the world and to touch the images in our minds with an ineffable beauty, then poetry is a momentary harmony in the soul amid stagnation or conflict — a glimpse of the divine and an incitation to the religious life.... Religion is poetry become the guide of life, poetry substituted for science, or supervening upon it as an approach to the highest reality. Poetry is religion allowed to drift, left without points of application in conduct and without expression in worship and dogma; it is religion without practical efficiency and without metaphysical illusion.

Mr. Masefield, in an address on poetry given in 1931, brings great poetry into even closer touch with the Supreme Reality:

> I would say that it [poetry] is a touching of the Life of the Universe, a lifting into the Universal Mood.... The greater poetry is a flowing in of light from the source of all light, from that King from whom comes all our knowledge of the kingly, in whose wisdom we advance, under whose majesty we move, and in whose beauty, if we have cared for beauty, we may come to dwell. His ways are ways of light; His words are words of light, vouchsafed to a few great men of light, so that this world may know a little of the wisdom, beauty, and power which are the daily bread in Paradise.

The Great Poets and the Meaning of Life

These rapt words are surely not a definition of poetry; they are the ardent testimony of a citizen of that realm. Poetry is a mood, a shining vision into the Life of the Universe, and the great poet makes the vision manifest and sets down its truth. Substitute the word 'religion' for the word 'poetry' in Masefield's description and every radiant saint in the calendar of the Church would consider it a noble and acceptable witness to the glories of religion.

The Distinctive Teachings of this Epic of Redemption

In ending the previous chapters I have summarized the principal teachings of the work under discussion, but in a study of the English Bible the conditions are different. Is it too much to assume that the reader is so familiar with the book that a summary is superfluous? Besides, who could make it? It would be like attempting to itemize the wealth of a continent in a few sentences. It is possible, however, to indicate some of those values which distinguish this epic from the epics and dramas we have considered.

In its conception of the nature of the Ultimate Reality, the Creative and Sustaining Power, the Most High, it presents a marked contrast. The Ultimate Energy in Homer was Fate, tempered by the activities of the Olympians. The God of Aeschylus was a moral governor, august in righteousness, whose memory of guilt was long. The gods of Lucretius were unaffected by the woes of men, and unhelpful, except indirectly. The Ultimate Reality was the atom, lapped in universal law, unconscious and without purpose. Virgil's Supreme Being was a nobler Caesar, ruling in the interests of peace and justice.

The men of the higher spiritual consciousness among the Hebrews interpreted the Most High, not through nature and her processes, but through man and his experiences. They found him in the events of their history and in the 'still, small, voice.' He was a god merciful and righteous, 'slow to anger and plenteous in mercy, who would by no means clear the guilty,' visiting, indeed, the iniquities of the fathers upon the children even to the third and fourth generation, but showing mercy for a thousand generations. This noblest conception of the Old Testament moves upward in the New Testament to the more intimate sense of the Father, just and compassionate.

The Scriptures declare that this great God was in the beginning, is in all the process, and will be at the consummation. The conviction that God is good and that his purposes stand sure brought a glorious hope into the world. Life is worth while and the possibilities of the future radiant beyond imagination. In no other epic is hope so dominant and exultant. Dante under the spell of this vision did not write a Divine Tragedy, but the *Divine Comedy*, for man by the grace of God can win a complete victory over evil powers.

No book in literature has done so much to persuade man of his essential greatness and unplumbed possibilities. The breath of God is in his nostrils; he is infinitely dear to the Most High. A mother may forget her sucking child, but he is not forgotten; the hairs of his head are numbered;

he abides under the shadow of the Almighty. He has but to obey and follow the Hero and all things work for his good; his present sufferings are not worthy to be compared with the glory that shall be revealed in him. He will come out of the battle more than conqueror, a perfected and shining spirit conformed to the likeness of his Hero. When Dante visits the realms of the dead, he does not find pitiable ghosts. As he enters Paradise the spirits of the redeemed are so glorious that his mortal eyes could not discern their lineaments. They appeared to him pillars of splendor. No other book has stimulated such faith in the spiritual potentialities of man.

The virtues which this Hebrew-Christian epic enjoins are in strong contrast to the qualities exalted in the others. The loftiest imperative of the Greeks was reason; that of the Scriptures is faith issuing in love. The classic world emphasized the sovereignty of the intellect; the Hebrews went more deeply into human nature, claiming that a clean heart is the primary necessity. Humility and a contrite heart receive more honor than militant self-reliance.

The conquering force exhibited in this book is not such courageous might as Achilles exemplified, nor the wisdom of crafty Ulysses. Not might nor power, but spiritual influences will completely subdue the enemy. Sacrificial love is the might against which naught avails. This is the 'arm of the Lord' which astonished Isaiah. John was amazed when, instead of the Lion of the tribe of Judah, he saw a Lamb as it had been slain seated in the center of the throne. This is the deep and eternal meaning of the

Cross. Love, not valor, not even reason is the trustiest weapon in this warfare with hostile powers.

The duration of the adventure and its consummation are on a scale befitting a world epic. The struggle lasts, not for ten or twenty years, but from the Creation until time shall be no more. And the goal is not the fall of a city, or the return of a single wanderer; it is a perfected society, a kingdom of God, established either in this world, or in that which is to come. This epic certainly ends in a blaze of splendor which is approached by no other. The sweep and passion and grandeur of the ages are in it.

In the literature of power this epic is supreme. It has moulded civilizations and turned the stream of the centuries to an extent and with a beneficence which is not approached by the combined influence of all the epics and dramas we have considered. To multitudes in many ages and in many countries it seems so close to the heart of things that it is the veritable Word of God. Now the designation, 'Word of God,' does not necessarily imply the language of God; it means the disclosure of God, the touch of the Eternal on the spirit of man. In the classic authors we have studied, the gods appear and speak as part of the machinery of the play, but Fate, the Ultimate Reality, preserves an awful silence. Silent is Dante's Point, and silent also the Mystery which formed the background of Shakespeare's tragedies. It is true, Chalcas and Tiresias could read events in the mind of Fate, but the awful Power kept in the shadow and in the silence.

But in this epic the Final Reality is active. His will is

vivid in the mind of his prophets. They speak confidently, 'Thus saith the Lord'; again he speaks directly to his people: 'Wash you, make you clean; put away the evil of your doings before mine eyes.' Dante, in the *Comedy*, could confidently affirm,

> There is a light above, which visible
> Makes the Creator unto every creature,
> Whom only in beholding Him has peace.

This is beautiful, but it lacks the moving power of the direct speech of this epic, 'Look unto me and be ye saved, all the ends of the earth: for I am God and there is none else.' But the Eternal does not merely utter his voice from the Mystery; he comes upon the stage. Men behold his glory, full of grace and truth. In the Scriptures the Supernatural does not seem to be the setting of the drama, the background; it is the power and wisdom pervading all thought and action. It is more intimate, more convincing and impressive than in any of the great masterpieces of literature. The marvelous story is told with a simplicity, a clarity, and an absoluteness of conviction which causes men to feel a Presence, a touch of the Unseen which seems to them to be authentic. The Deep without stirs the Deep that is within. This power to make the story seem to men an authentic disclosure of the meaning of life and the sources of refreshment is peculiar to the Scriptures. No epic has ever so completely performed the service of great literature, giving to multitudes peace, liberty, spiritual elation.

What is Common to All

BEFORE seeking to learn the truths which all the poets either took for granted, admired, or affirmed, let us take a brief glance at the truths and values emphasized by each. The virtue which Homer has made shining and unforgettable is courage. The conditions of life are hard and pathetic, but a man should heroically confront his fate and through valor achieve glory.

With Aeschylus we associate the grandeur and precision of the moral law. One evil begets a chain of evils which cause suffering both to the innocent and the guilty. The chain is broken when a good man or a god takes the burden vicariously upon himself.

Lucretius has served the world by lifting up a thrilling vision of a universe in which caprice and fear have no part; they are expelled by universal law. If one would remedy an evil, let him find the cause and remove it.

Virgil, living in the Golden Age and close to the seat of power, read the meaning of life in terms of national destiny. Like the prophets of Israel, he discerned the will of the Supreme working through the centuries of human struggle for peace and justice to all men.

Dante, as the loftiest and more comprehensive poet of

Christianity, shifts the emphasis of his thought from physical warfare to the aspirations of the spirit. He shows the way by which men may bring their desires and will into perfect harmony with the Love that moves all things. He proclaims the way to turn darkest tragedy into divine comedy: by discipline to achieve victory.

Shakespeare's peculiar contribution is most difficult to characterize. Broadly speaking it is a revelation of the variety, the meaning, the fascination of human life, through a wizardry of art which seldom fails to awaken wonder.

The uniqueness of the world epic disclosed in the Scriptures is the Divine Hero ever suffering, ever conquering through the power of sacrificial love. Through the ages by his agony and bloody sweat he is winning a perfect victory over evil and all its effects.

These peculiarities have all been noted in the preceding pages. Of much more interest and not so immediately evident are the truths these poets assume in common and the virtues they all admire. The student of literature can scarcely fail to remark that these master minds seem to appear at a destined hour, at a focal point where many forces are meeting preparatory to some momentous epoch. The greatness is not entirely in the poet who sings the truths of the epoch; the period is momentous and inspiring. All of these poets whom we have been studying came at a time when one of the most important languages was either coming to the fullness of its glory, or else was in full flower. Words were living things, sentences were plastic, speech was revealing its wonders, and people took delight in it.

What is Common to All

Homer found a language made melodious by many singers; Aeschylus came at the hour when Athenian genius was awakening to the beauty and meaning of the world. And his actors made up for the lack of stage machinery by pronouncing their lines with loving distinctness. Lucretius did much to smooth the strength of the Latin to beauty, and Virgil subdued the speech of Rome to express the finer shadings of emotion. Dante came of a school of poets who sang in the 'sweet, new style,' and by his ability to make the flexible words carry the burden of his thought became the chief moulder of the Italian speech. The great poets of Palestine form a succession from the beginning to the decline of the Hebrew tongue. The greatest came in the golden hour of the Hebrew language.

These poets serve as monuments marking the progress of the race; they commemorate its momentous turning points — they sum up one period and usher in another, erecting at the same time a standard of excellence to measure its achievements.

They are all affirmative, they are distinguished for a magnificence of faith, for creative genius by its very nature believes and asserts. So far as the great poets are sceptical it is of some superstition, some outworn theory, some non-essential idea. Their total effect leaves the reader in an elevated mood, not rebellious or hopeless.

They all declare that valor, magnanimity, honor, adherence to duty, self-control, are more in accord with what lies at the heart of things than self-glorification.

They agree that something is wrong with the world and that the evil has its source in some form of self-love — in pride, lust, ambition, ungoverned passions. To the Greeks the root of sin is excess; Dante calls it loving the wrong objects; Shakespeare builds his tragedies on the fatal tendency of men to identify themselves totally with one interest. The universe is against this. A law not of today nor of yesterday, 'whose seat is in the bosom of God and whose voice is the harmony of the world' exacts expiation; the evildoer must pay; the harvest will follow the sowing.

But evil and punishment are not the final words. 'Wisdom comes through suffering,' 'The wrath of man shall praise thee,' wrote both the ancient Hebrew and Greek poets. The 'benefit of ill' was one of Shakespeare's dearly bought convictions. And Virgil insists that Roman virtue and grandeur were earned by many and great struggles.

It was also a common faith with them that human fortunes are not determined by the whim or the anger of the gods, but that one's character influences one's destiny. What destroys the hero is not some alien force, but some weakness or exaggerated passion within himself. He is not lacking in responsibility for his fate.

Writing these pages one's pen is constantly checked by a sense of the massive figure of Lucretius standing by, and the realization of the questioning look which occasionally comes to his face. My answer to him is this: 'You were a tremendous believer, you lived by faith, you ennobled men's thoughts, you gave them courage and a wonderful vision. Doubtless your philosophy of evil and the human will would be stated in different words from those used by those others who stand in the Great Succession, but you were like them in your love of beauty and virtue and behaved toward evil in much the same way. Like them you acted as a responsible being.'

All of these poets, including emphatically Lucretius, had a vivid sense of the Infinite and Eternal Power; they thought of this as working against what we call wrong and re-enforcing what we call right. Ultimate harmony was the *summum bonum* of life in the thought of all; they touch its many aspects; they think of it as peace, reconciliation, liberty, virtue come to full vitality and luster; without exception they believed that help comes from the Invisible to the open spirit of man.

The poets who dealt most extensively with human struggles in the extreme moments stress most insistently and powerfully that there is a quality in the human spirit that is superior to disaster, that 'feeds on death,' that is sublimely above all the reaches of the malignity of evil, that distills wisdom from sorrow, finds wells of refreshment in the darkest valleys, extracts beauty from ashes and oil from the flinty rocks of difficulty. Dante teaches this by the whole movement of his journey through hell to the *visio Dei*; Aeschylus and Shakespeare embody this conviction in far-shining characters; the Scriptures reiterate it from the Garden of Eden to the celestial City of God.

This consciousness that life as it is on the earth is a battle field of vigilant and hostile forces, that man is confronted by many great dangers, calling for discipline, control, high courage, pity, and magnanimity, is common to all. Common also is the belief that through the exercise of his moral will man can live spiritually victorious when his fortunes and his hopes lie in utter ruin. Common is the belief in help from the Unseen, and the sense that the meaning of life has not been fully disclosed during the years of our mortality.

Of these virtues and faiths the poets have been the chief teachers; they have transmitted them from generation to generation and from civilization to civilization. They have thus not only taught the supreme truths; they have unified humanity by giving men sympathetic understanding of other days and other battles; they bring old experience to mature the mind of the race.

THE END

Index

Index